INTRODUCING
ISSUES WITH
OPPOSING
VIEWPOINTS®

Afghanistan

Lauri S. Friedman, *Book Editor*

GREENHAVEN PRESS
A part of Gale, Cengage Learning

GALE
CENGAGE Learning™

Detroit • New York • San Francisco • New Haven, Conn • Waterville, Maine • London

Christine Nasso, *Publisher*
Elizabeth Des Chenes, *Managing Editor*

For more information, contact:
Greenhaven Press
27500 Drake Rd.
Farmington Hills, MI 48331-3535
Or you can visit our Internet site at gale.cengage.com

For product information and technology assistance, contact us at

Gale Customer Support, 1-800-877-4253
For permission to use material from this text or product, submit all requests online at www.cengage.com/permissions

Further permissions questions can be e-mailed to permissionrequest@cengage.com

Articles in Greenhaven Press anthologies are often edited for length to meet page requirements. In addition, original titles of these works are changed to clearly present the main thesis and to explicitly indicate the author's opinion. Every effort is made to ensure that Greenhaven Press accurately reflects the original intent of the authors. Every effort has been made to trace the owners of copyrighted material.

Cover image copyright © Zaheerudin/Webistan/Corbis.

LIBRARY OF CONGRESS CATALOGING-IN-PUBLICATION DATA

Afghanistan / Lauri S. Friedman, book editor.
   p. cm. -- (Introducing issues with opposing viewpoints)
  Includes bibliographical references and index.
  ISBN 978-0-7377-4729-4 (hardcover)
  1. Afghan War, 2001---Juvenile literature. 2. Afghan War, 2001---United States--Juvenile literature. 3. Afghanistan--Politics and government--2001---Juvenile literature.
I. Friedman, Lauri S.
  DS371.412.A36 2010
  958.104'7--dc22

                             2009050776

Printed in the United States of America
1 2 3 4 5 6 7 14 13 12 11 10

Contents

Chapter 3: How Should the United States Proceed in Afghanistan?

Foreword

Indulging in a wide spectrum of ideas, beliefs, and perspectives is a critical cornerstone of democracy. After all, it is often debates over differences of opinion, such as whether to legalize abortion, how to treat prisoners, or when to enact the death penalty, that shape our society and drive it forward. Such diversity of thought is frequently regarded as the hallmark of a healthy and civilized culture. As the Reverend Clifford Schutjer of the First Congregational Church in Mansfield, Ohio, declared in a 2001 sermon, "Surrounding oneself with only like-minded people, restricting what we listen to or read only to what we find agreeable is irresponsible. Refusing to entertain doubts once we make up our minds is a subtle but deadly form of arrogance." With this advice in mind, Introducing Issues with Opposing Viewpoints books aim to open readers' minds to the critically divergent views that comprise our world's most important debates.

Introducing Issues with Opposing Viewpoints simplifies for students the enormous and often overwhelming mass of material now available via print and electronic media. Collected in every volume is an array of opinions that captures the essence of a particular controversy or topic. Introducing Issues with Opposing Viewpoints books embody the spirit of nineteenth-century journalist Charles A. Dana's axiom: "Fight for your opinions, but do not believe that they contain the whole truth, or the only truth." Absorbing such contrasting opinions teaches students to analyze the strength of an argument and compare it to its opposition. From this process readers can inform and strengthen their own opinions, or be exposed to new information that will change their minds. Introducing Issues with Opposing Viewpoints is a mosaic of different voices. The authors are statesmen, pundits, academics, journalists, corporations, and ordinary people who have felt compelled to share their experiences and ideas in a public forum. Their words have been collected from newspapers, journals, books, speeches, interviews, and the Internet, the fastest growing body of opinionated material in the world.

Introducing Issues with Opposing Viewpoints shares many of the well-known features of its critically acclaimed parent series, Opposing Viewpoints. The articles are presented in a pro/con format, allowing readers to absorb divergent perspectives side by side. Active reading questions preface each viewpoint, requiring the student to approach the material thoughtfully and carefully. Useful charts, graphs, and cartoons supplement each article. A thorough introduction provides readers with crucial background on an issue. An annotated bibliography points the reader toward articles, books, and Web sites that contain additional information on the topic. An appendix of organizations to contact contains a wide variety of charities, nonprofit organizations, political groups, and private enterprises that each hold a position on the issue at hand. Finally, a comprehensive index allows readers to locate content quickly and efficiently.

Introducing Issues with Opposing Viewpoints is also significantly different from Opposing Viewpoints. As the series title implies, its presentation will help introduce students to the concept of opposing viewpoints and learn to use this material to aid in critical writing and debate. The series' four-color, accessible format makes the books attractive and inviting to readers of all levels. In addition, each viewpoint has been carefully edited to maximize a reader's understanding of the content. Short but thorough viewpoints capture the essence of an argument. A substantial, thought-provoking essay question placed at the end of each viewpoint asks the student to further investigate the issues raised in the viewpoint, compare and contrast two authors' arguments, or consider how one might go about forming an opinion on the topic at hand. Each viewpoint contains sidebars that include at-a-glance information and handy statistics. A Facts About section located in the back of the book further supplies students with relevant facts and figures.

Following in the tradition of the Opposing Viewpoints series, Greenhaven Press continues to provide readers with invaluable exposure to the controversial issues that shape our world. As John Stuart Mill once wrote: "The only way in which a human being can make some approach to knowing the whole of a subject is by hearing what can be said about it by persons of every variety of opinion and studying all modes in which it can be looked at by every character of mind. No wise man ever acquired his wisdom in any mode but this." It is to this principle that Introducing Issues with Opposing Viewpoints books are dedicated.

Introduction

Many problems are faced by U.S. and international forces struggling to quell terrorism and install peace and democracy in Afghanistan. One major issue is the drug trade: Afghanistan is the leading global supplier of opium, a by-product of the poppy plant, which is used to make heroin. Afghanistan's drug trade has become an increasing problem since the United States invaded in 2001 and is critically tied to whether U.S. and international troops can succeed in their mission there.

Opium production had long been a problem in Afghanistan, but a little over a year prior to the U.S. invasion, Taliban leaders clamped down significantly on the industry, banning opium cultivation and production in the country. The Taliban ruled with such tight control that farmers had little choice but to obey the ban. Therefore, very little planting of poppies was done in 2000. As a result, the spring 2001 harvest was the lowest on recent record for Afghanistan, with opium production close to zero.

But when the United States toppled the Taliban in October of 2001, it unwittingly unleashed Afghanistan's opium industry. With little or no control established in the country, warlords were free to resume opium production—and they did so at a faster rate than ever before. According to the Strategic Studies Institute, an institute of the U.S. military, by 2004 the opium harvest set record highs; by 2006 production was double the amount it had been in the late 1990s. As of 2009, Afghanistan was by far the world's largest producer of opium: That year the United Nations estimated Afghanistan produced 92 percent of the global supply and generated $65 billion, most of which went to fund terrorism globally. And, despite the presence of thousands of foreign troops there for more than eight years, corruption, violence, and lawlessness continue to prevent 98 percent of opium from being seized at the Afghan borders.

Afghan farmers grow poppies and participate in the drug trade for several reasons, most of them economic. A 2009 report by the United Nations Office on Drugs and Crime (UNODC) found that 53 percent of Afghan farmers say they grow opium because of the high price it fetches on the global market. Another 32 percent say it helps alleviate their poverty. Indeed, most Afghans are very poor, and their harsh landscape, war-torn country, and unstable government make opportunities for income few and far between. This is the reason many of them turn to poppy production. As John A. Glaze of the Strategic Studies Institute says, "Cultivating opium poppy makes powerful economic sense to the impoverished farmers of Afghanistan. It is the easiest crop to grow and the most profitable."[1] In fact, the Strategic Studies Institute estimates that an Afghan farmer can make seventeen times more money growing opium poppies than he can growing wheat.

Poppies are also drought resistant, easy to transport, withstand long-term storage, and do not require refrigeration. "With Afghanistan's limited irrigation, electricity, roads, and other infrastructure, growing traditional crops can be extremely difficult," explains Glaze. "In many cases, farmers are simply unable to support their families growing traditional crops; and because most rural farmers are uneducated and illiterate, they have few economically viable alternatives to growing opium poppy."[2] This is the reason that by the end of 2007, a record 2.9 million Afghans from twenty-eight of thirty-four provinces—or nearly 10 percent of the population—were involved in some form of opium production.

Afghanistan's drug trade has posed significant problems for the United States and international soldiers fighting the war there. According to the UNODC, drug-related funds supply Taliban insurgents and warlords with between $95 and $160 million dollars per year, sometimes more if a crop is particularly healthy (from 2006–2007, for example, the Taliban was estimated to have earned between $200–$400 million from the drug trade). These funds are spent keeping the Taliban supplied with weaponry and other materials they use to launch attacks on U.S. and international forces and Afghan government officials.

One way money from the drug trade is used is to pay Afghans to side with the Taliban rather than with U.S. and North Atlantic Treaty Organization [NATO] troops. For example, the U.S. military reports that the Taliban use drug money to pay Afghan men up to two hundred dollars a month to fight with them. Afghan police officers, on the other hand, who are charged with protecting the Afghan government and working with U.S. and NATO troops, are paid only seventy dollars per month. To struggling Afghans, then, working with the Taliban rather than against them is much more profitable. That the Taliban are able to buy Afghans' loyalty with drug money has been a major reason that ousting them from the country, and installing law and order, has been so challenging for troops.

Money from the drug trade has also made corruption widespread in the Afghan government. It is reported that farmers routinely bribe police, law enforcement, and other Afghan officials to ignore or even protect activity related to the drug trade. In 2006 the *Washington Post* and the *New York Times* reported that Afghan government officials were involved in at least 70 percent of opium trafficking, and as many as 25 percent of parliament members were suspected of involvement in the drug trade. President Hamid Karzai—himself accused of corruption—has said that "drugs in Afghanistan are threatening the very existence of the Afghan State."[3] The UNODC confirmed in 2009 that "the drugs trade remains a major source of revenue for anti-government forces and organized crime operating in and around Afghanistan. Drug money is also a lubricant for corruption that contaminates power."[4]

As of 2009, some good news was discovered about the opium trade in Afghanistan. An October report from the UNODC found that Afghanistan's opium cultivation was down 22 percent from 2008. Production was particularly low in southern and western parts of the country. When asked why they had stopped planting poppy plants, farmers gave several answers. Some said they stopped participating in the drug trade because it is against Islam, while others felt increased pressure to stop from government authorities. A few said a drought had made poppy growth more difficult. But the majority said they stopped because the increased sale price of wheat made it more profitable to plant that crop than it had been in previous years. While farmers can still earn more growing opium than wheat, the price gap between the two crops has narrowed substantially as a result of high amounts of opium already available on the global market. Indeed, in 2009 the UNODC reported that opium prices had dropped by about 40 percent and were at their lowest level since the late 1990s. UN and Afghan officials were trying to take advantage of this development by encouraging farmers to pursue wheat and other benign crops under a new $300 million program supported by the Agency for International Development.

However, although opium prices fell and cultivation was down, the problem was far from being resolved. It was reported that Afghan poppy crops are being grown more efficiently than ever before, so that each hectare of poppies now yields about 15 percent more opium than in years past. Furthermore, farmers have become more adept at hiding their opium stocks from the military, putting them in underground storage containers rather than aboveground warehouses and shacks. Finally, even a reduced amount of drug trafficking still results in millions of dollars being diverted to terrorist insurgents and Taliban leadership.

How Afghanistan's drug trade has hampered the U.S. war effort there is one of the many topics explored in *Introducing Issues with Opposing Viewpoints: Afghanistan*. Readers will also consider arguments about whether more U.S. troops should be sent there, whether Afghanistan can ever be turned into a democracy, and whether the war there is just. Readers will examine these questions in the viewpoint pairs and make their own decisions about what U.S. policy should be toward this troubled nation.

Notes

1. John A. Glaze, "Opium and Afghanistan: Reassessing U.S. Counternarcotics Strategy," Strategic Studies Institute, October 2007, p. 5. www.strategicstudiesinstitute.army.mil/pdffiles/pub 804.pdf.

2. Glaze, "Opium and Afghanistan, p. 5.

3. Quoted in Anne Barnard and Farah Stockman, "U.S. Weighs Role in Heroin War in Afghanistan," *Boston Globe*, October 20, 2004.

4. United Nations Office on Drugs and Crime, "Afghanistan: Opium Winter Assessment," January 2009, p. 5. www.unodc.org/docu ments/crop-monitoring/ORA_report_2009.pdf.

Chapter 1

What Is the Status of the War in Afghanistan?

After years of war in Afghanistan, whether the United States can restore order and defeat terrorism there has become the subject of much debate.

Afghanistan Is a Just War

Barack Obama

"We are in Afghanistan to confront a common enemy that threatens the United States, our friends and our allies, and the people of Afghanistan."

In the following viewpoint Barack Obama explains why the war in Afghanistan is a just undertaking. He reminds Americans that the war in Afghanistan began because the terrorists who attacked the United States on September 11, 2001, operated from inside Afghanistan. These groups remain a threat to the United States and the world, and so Obama says they must be eliminated. Furthermore, Obama says that if the United States does not fight in Afghanistan, that country's citizens—particularly its women and girls—will be subject to perpetual violence and a denial of their basic human rights. For all of these reasons, Obama believes that war in Afghanistan is not a luxury but a necessity.

Obama is the forty-fourth president of the United States.

AS YOU READ, CONSIDER THE FOLLOWING QUESTIONS:

1. Who is Ayman al-Zawahiri, and what does Obama say he has done?
2. What cities does Obama say have suffered terrorist attacks that were plotted from inside either Afghanistan or Pakistan?
3. How many Americans have died fighting thus far in Afghanistan, according to Obama?

Barack Obama, "Remarks by the President on a New Strategy for Afghanistan and Pakistan," The White House, Office of the Press Secretary, March 27, 2009.

The situation [in Afghanistan] is increasingly perilous. It's been more than seven years since the Taliban was removed from power, yet war rages on, and insurgents control parts of Afghanistan and Pakistan. Attacks against our troops, our NATO [North Atlantic Treaty Organization] allies, and the Afghan government have risen steadily. And most painfully, 2008 was the deadliest year of the war for American forces.

Many people in the United States—and many in partner countries that have sacrificed so much—have a simple question: What is our purpose in Afghanistan? After so many years, they ask, why do our men and women still fight and die there? And they deserve a straightforward answer.

Our Worst Enemy Resides in Afghanistan

So let me be clear: Al Qaeda and its allies—the terrorists who planned and supported the 9/11 attacks—are in Pakistan and Afghanistan. Multiple intelligence estimates have warned that al Qaeda is actively planning attacks on the United States homeland from its safe haven in Pakistan. And if the Afghan government falls to the Taliban—or allows al Qaeda to go unchallenged—that country will again be a base for terrorists who want to kill as many of our people as they possibly can.

The future of Afghanistan is inextricably linked to the future of its neighbor, Pakistan. In the nearly eight years since 9/11, al Qaeda and its extremist allies have moved across the border to the remote areas of the Pakistani frontier. This almost certainly includes al Qaeda's leadership: Osama bin Laden and Ayman al-Zawahiri. They have used this mountainous terrain as a safe haven to hide, to train terrorists, to communicate with followers, to plot attacks, and to send fighters to support the insurgency in Afghanistan. For the American people, this border region has become the most dangerous place in the world.

Afghanistan Poses an International Threat

But this is not simply an American problem—far from it. It is, instead, an international security challenge of the highest order. Terrorist attacks in London and Bali were tied to al Qaeda and its allies in Pakistan, as were attacks in North Africa and the Middle East, in Islamabad and in Kabul. If there is a major attack on an

Asian, European, or African city, it, too, is likely to have ties to al Qaeda's leadership in Pakistan. The safety of people around the world is at stake.

The Afghan People Need Us

For the Afghan people, a return to Taliban rule would condemn their country to brutal governance, international isolation, a paralyzed economy, and the denial of basic human rights to the Afghan people—especially women and girls. The return in force of al Qaeda terrorists who would accompany the core Taliban leadership would cast Afghanistan under the shadow of perpetual violence.

As President, my greatest responsibility is to protect the American people. We are not in Afghanistan to control that country or to dictate its future. We are in Afghanistan to confront a common enemy that threatens the United States, our friends and our allies, and the people of Afghanistan and Pakistan who have suffered the most at the hands of violent extremists.

A Clear, Focused Goal

So I want the American people to understand that we have a clear and focused goal: to disrupt, dismantle and defeat al Qaeda in Pakistan

U.S. President Barack Obama, with members of his cabinet behind him, makes remarks about a comprehensive new strategy for Afghanistan and Pakistan in 2009.

and Afghanistan, and to prevent their return to either country in the future. That's the goal that must be achieved. That is a cause that could not be more just. And to the terrorists who oppose us, my message is the same: We will defeat you.

To achieve our goals, we need a stronger, smarter and comprehensive strategy. To focus on the greatest threat to our people, America must no longer deny resources to Afghanistan because of the war in Iraq. . . .

"A Shared Responsibility to Act"

Going forward, we will not blindly stay the course. Instead, we will set clear metrics to measure progress and hold ourselves accountable. We'll consistently assess our efforts to train Afghan security forces and our progress in combating insurgents. We will measure the growth of Afghanistan's economy, and its illicit narcotics production. And we will review whether we are using the right tools and tactics to make progress towards accomplishing our goals.

None of the steps that I've outlined will be easy; none should be taken by America alone. The world cannot afford the price that will come due if Afghanistan slides back into chaos or al Qaeda operates unchecked. We have a shared responsibility to act—not because we seek to project power for its own sake, but because our own peace and security depends on it. And what's at stake at this time is not just our own security—it's the very idea that free nations can come together on behalf of our common security. That was the founding cause of NATO six decades ago, and that must be our common purpose today. . . .

That is true, above all, for the coalition that has fought together in Afghanistan, side by side with Afghans. The sacrifices have been enormous. Nearly 700 Americans have lost their lives.

Troops from over 20 countries have also paid the ultimate price. All Americans honor the service and cherish the friendship of those who have fought, and worked, and bled by our side.

> **FAST FACT**
>
> The September 11, 2001, terrorist attacks killed 2,973 people. The attacks were executed by terrorists who were mostly from Saudi Arabia but who trained inside Afghanistan.

Who Is Fighting in Afghanistan?

Although forty-two countries have committed troops to Afghanistan, soldiers from nine countries do most of the fighting.

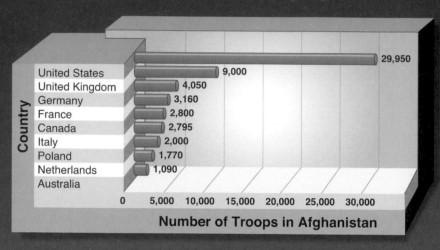

Taken from: NATO HQ Media Operations Centre, July 2009.

And all Americans are awed by the service of our own men and women in uniform, who've borne a burden as great as any other generation's. They and their families embody the example of selfless sacrifice.

We Did Not Choose This War

I remind everybody, the United States of America did not choose to fight a war in Afghanistan. Nearly 3,000 of our people were killed on September 11, 2001, for doing nothing more than going about their daily lives. Al Qaeda and its allies have since killed thousands of people in many countries. Most of the blood on their hands is the blood of Muslims, who al Qaeda has killed and maimed in far greater number than any other people. That is the future that al Qaeda is offering to the people of Pakistan and Afghanistan—a future without hope or opportunity; a future without justice or peace.

So understand, the road ahead will be long and there will be difficult days ahead. But we will seek lasting partnerships with Afghanistan and Pakistan that promise a new day for their people. And we will use all elements of our national power to defeat al Qaeda, and to defend America, our allies, and all who seek a better future. Because the United States of America stands for peace and security, justice and opportunity. That is who we are, and that is what history calls on us to do once more.

EVALUATING THE AUTHOR'S ARGUMENTS:

Obama says the war in Afghanistan is just in part because America did not choose to fight it—the United States was attacked on September 11 and thus has the right to defend itself. Do you agree with him? Does the fact that America was attacked by terrorists who used Afghanistan as a planning base make the war in Afghanistan just? Why or why not?

Viewpoint

2

Afghanistan Is Not a Just War

Ted Rall

"It has long been an article of faith . . . that Afghanistan is the 'good war,' a righteous campaign. . . . But the facts say otherwise."

Afghanistan is not a justifiable or winnable war, argues Ted Rall in the following viewpoint. He says that much of the justification for the war in Afghanistan comes from the idea that the September 11 terrorists plotted from that country—yet Rall suggests that the main plotters worked not out of Afghanistan but Egypt. For this reason, Rall thinks Afghanistan is the wrong target if the reason for fighting is revenge for September 11. In addition, Rall thinks the war in Afghanistan is unwinnable. The country is larger and more remote than Iraq, which has proven difficult to win in even with more troops and money than have been spent in Afghanistan. Rall says that Afghanistan has been wrongly billed as the "good war"—and because it is not justifiable or winnable, Rall thinks America should not put any more effort into fighting there.

Rall is the author of the book *Silk Road to Run: Is Central Asia the New Middle East?*

AS YOU READ, CONSIDER THE FOLLOWING QUESTIONS:

1. What terrorist organization does Rall say likely recruited the 9/11 terrorists?
2. What does the word *tertiary* mean in the context of the viewpoint?
3. How many troops does the author say have been sent to Iraq? How many have been sent to Afghanistan?

F ive years after the Republicans got us into war against Iraq, Democrats want to double down on a war that's even more unjustifiable and unwinnable—the one against Afghanistan. By any measure, U.S. troops and their NATO allies are getting their asses kicked in the country that Reagan's CIA station chief for Pakistan called "the graveyard of empires." Afghanistan currently produces a record 93 percent of the world's opium. Suicide bombers are killing more U.S.-aligned troops than ever. Stonings are back. The Taliban and their allies, "defeated" in 2001, control most of the country—and may recapture the capital of Kabul as early as this summer.

"So," asks *The New York Times*, "has Afghanistan now become a bigger security threat to the United States than Iraq?" Barack Obama's answer is yes. He spent last year parroting the DNC's line that Bush "took his eye off the ball" in Afghanistan when we invaded Iraq. Thankfully, he abandoned that hoary sports metaphor. Iraq, he says now, "distracted us from the fight that needed to be fought in Afghanistan against Al Qaeda. They're the ones who killed 3,000 Americans."

Sorta. But not really.

Osama bin Laden bragged about ordering the East Africa embassy bombings in 1998, yet has repeatedly denied a direct role in 9/11. He's probably telling the truth. The hijackers were mostly likely

FAST FACT

A July 2009 Gallup poll found that 61 percent of Americans believe that going to war in Afghanistan was a mistake.

Americans Are Worried the War in Afghanistan Was a Mistake

Each year, more Americans say they think it was a mistake to send military forces to Afghanistan after the September 11, 2001, attacks.

"Do you think the United States made a mistake in sending military forces to Afghanistan in October 2001, or not?"

Date	Made a Mistake %	Did Not Make a Mistake %	Unsure %
September 2009	37	61	2
July 2008	28	68	4
August 2007	25	70	5
July 2004	25	72	3
January 2002	6	93	1
November 2001	9	89	2

Taken from: Gallup poll, August 31–September 2, 2009.

recruited by Islamic Jihad, which is based in Egypt. Saudis, including members of the royal family, financed the strikes against New York and Washington. Pakistani intelligence funded and supervised the camps where some of them trained.

Al Qaeda may have been peripherally involved in 9/11; its leadership certainly knew about the plot ahead of time. They may have fronted some of the expense money. But 9/11 wasn't an Al Qaeda operation per se.

Afghanistan's connection to 9/11 was tertiary. At the moment the first plane struck the South Tower of the World Trade Center, most of Al Qaeda's camps and fighters were in Pakistan. As CBS News reported on January 29, 2002, Osama bin Laden was in a Pakistani military hospital in Rawalpindi on 9/11. The Taliban militia, which provided neither men nor money for the attacks, controlled 90 percent of the country.

It has long been an article of faith among Democrats that Afghanistan is the "good war," a righteous campaign that could be won with more money and manpower. But the facts say otherwise. The U.S. Air Force rained more than a million pounds of bombs upon Afghanistan in 2007, mostly on innocent civilians. It's twice as much as was dropped in Iraq—and equally ineffective.

Six years after the U.S. invasion of 2001, according to Director of National Intelligence Michael McConnell, the U.S./NATO occupation force has surged from 8,000 to 50,000. But the Americans are having no more luck against the Afghans than had the Brits or the Soviet Union. The U.S.-backed government of Hamid Karzai controls a mere 30 percent of Afghanistan, admits McConnell. (Regional analysts say in truth it is closer to 15 percent.) Most of the country belongs to the charming guys who gave us babes in burqas and exploding Buddhas: the Taliban and likeminded warlords. "Afghanistan remains a failing state," says a report by General James Jones, former NATO Supreme Allied Commander. "The United States and the international community have tried to win the struggle in Afghanistan with too few military forces and insufficient economic aid."

If he becomes president, Obama says he'll "ask more from our European allies" to win in Afghanistan. But he won't get it. As *The New York Times* puts it: "Why help the United States in Afghanistan, the European logic goes, when America would be able to handle Afghanistan much more easily if its GIs weren't bogged down in Iraq?"

Obama says he would send two more American combat brigades—between 3,000 and 8,000 troops. If 158,000 troops can't subdue Iraq, how can 58,000 do the job in Afghanistan?

They can't.

Afghanistan's population is 19 percent larger than that of Iraq. Its area is 49 percent bigger, with infinitely rougher terrain. Obama's proposed "surgelet" would result in troop strength of less than one sixth of the 400,000 dictated by official U.S. counterinsurgency doctrine for a nation the size of Afghanistan.

Afghans say spring could mark the beginning of the end of the United States' first experiment in post-9/11 regime change. For more than a year, Taliban commanders have controlled the key Kabul-to-Kandahar highway. "On one convoy last year we were 40 vehicles and only 12 got through," Sadat Khan, a 25-year-old truck driver explained to the UK *Telegraph* as he pointed to "roughly patched bullet holes in the cab of his truck." Cops loyal to Karzai expect to be massacred. "Maybe we will lose 30 per cent of us this spring, maybe 60 per cent," police commander Mohammad Farid told the paper. He'd already been shot.

The Taliban say they'll retake Kabul this year and reestablish the Islamic fundamentalist government led by Mullah Omar. No one knows whether they'll succeed. But they've already begun to strangle the city of Kabul. They're destroying its nascent telecommunications infrastructure, driving out foreign NGOs and businesspeople with terrorist attacks, and cutting off access to the remaining highways. Talibs promise to continue to target NATO troops, betting that Canada and other members of the coalition will pull out under

Taliban fighters pose in Ghanzi, Afghanistan, on October 19, 2009. Estimates suggest that the Taliban controls at least 70 percent of the country.

pressure from antiwar voters. Bogged down in Iraq, the U.S. won't be able to send more soldiers to Afghanistan. Karzai's puppet regime won't last long.

If Obama is so eager to keep fighting Bush's wars, he'd be smarter to focus on the more winnable of the two: Iraq.

EVALUATING THE AUTHORS' ARGUMENTS:

Barack Obama and Ted Rall disagree on the role Afghanistan played in the September 11 attacks. After reading both viewpoints, what do you think Afghanistan's connection was? What pieces of evidence helped you make up your mind? Given this, do you think Afghanistan is a just war?

Important Progress Has Been Made in Afghanistan

Douglas Alexander

"In Helmand [Afghanistan], my Department is delivering jobs, infrastructure, health and education services."

Douglas Alexander is the secretary of state for international development in the British government. In the following viewpoint he describes the progress British troops have made in Helmand Province, a region in southern Afghanistan. International military operations there have brought tens of thousands of people under friendly Afghan government control, allowing commanders and local leaders there to create jobs, open schools, and provide health care for the people who live in that region. He says farmers have been persuaded to plant food rather than drugs, the majority of people have health care coverage, and women are beginning to see an increase in rights. Although Afghanistan still faces many military, political, and social challenges, Alexander offers Helmand Province as an example of how success can be achieved in Afghanistan when military operations are combined with social and political programs.

I n recent weeks, British, American and Afghan troops have been engaged in combat around Taliban strongholds in Helmand province [in Afghanistan].

Political Progress Amidst Violence

At the same time, across the border, hundreds of soldiers have lost their lives in Pakistan's offensive against militants in tribal areas and more than two million civilians in that country have been forced from their homes.

And yet at the same time, as I saw for myself when I met a group of first time voters in Musa Qala on Monday [July 27, 2009], across Afghanistan preparations are underway for Presidential elections in just three weeks time which will determine the political direction of the country for the next five years. . . .

Military Progress Has Been Made

Of course Afghanistan today remains a highly insecure and violent place. Whilst in the north and the west of the country the situation is relatively more secure, in the south of Afghanistan, the number of violent incidents has risen significantly this year.

The insurgency is being countered militarily by a series of recent operations which aim to clear areas from Taliban control, secure them from attack, and then enable the Afghan authorities to bring basic services such as access to justice to the local people.

In recent weeks, we have seen a concerted offensive by British and American troops in Helmand through Operation Panther's Claw and Operation Khanjar. Operation Panther's Claw—which launched five weeks ago in Helmand—has involved over 3,000 troops from the UK, Afghanistan, Denmark and Estonia. And as a result of the

Chinook helicopters land British troops in Afghanistan's Helmand Province in July 2009 as part of Operation Panther's Claw.

operation, up to 100,000 people—about 10% of the population of Helmand—will be brought back under Afghan government control.

The success of this operation will allow greater movement between the important centres of Lashkar Gah and Gereshk. It will allow many more people to be able to vote in the upcoming elections. And as Brigadier [General] Tim Radford, Commander of Task Force Helmand, told me earlier in the week, within 48 hours of ground being taken by British forces, civilian stabilisation experts were beginning their work in the Babaji area: engaging with key leaders, organising community shuras [councils] and beginning the task of providing cash for work programmes.

So military progress has been made. . . .

Improvements to Education

And in recent years, since the last elections, there has been some progress in delivering services that improved the lives of many Afghans. The UN estimates that five million refugees have been able to return home since 2001. This year's cereal harvest is likely to be a record. And, crucially, increasing numbers of girls and boys are going to school.

Education is of course a vital investment in the future of any community, but in Afghanistan it brings broader benefits to a society where insurgents are recruited among the illiterate and impoverished, and communities are isolated by generations of poverty and conflict.

So it is not coincidental that since 2007, the Taliban and its allies have bombed, burned or attacked more than 530 schools across the country. As Thomas Friedman described it in his *New York Times* column [in July 2009], "this is the real war of ideas". For Afghanistan is a country where, as the Education Minister told me, the insurgents still behead teachers to terrorise and intimidate them out of their work to educate girls. But just as the Taliban close schools down, we are helping Afghans to re-open them, as I saw for myself in Musa Qala on Monday. With international support, more than six million children are now enrolled in school in Afghanistan, up from nine hundred thousand boys under the Taliban when educating girls was deemed unlawful—and around a third of them are girls.

> **FAST FACT**
>
> According to UNICEF and the Afghan Ministry of Education, school enrollment has soared since the fall of the Taliban in 2001. More than 4.2 million children enrolled in school between 2001 and 2007. Thirty-five percent of students are female.

Improvements to Healthcare and Politics

Other services have improved too. Basic healthcare now covers 82% of the country. 40,000 more Afghan children will see their fifth birthdays than in 2002. And women are starting to play a more active part in Afghan society. To take just one example, over 60% of the 450,000

More than Half of Afghanistan Is Under Control

Although significant areas of Afghanistan are under enemy control or at high risk of coming under enemy control, nearly two-thirds of the country—or 62 percent—is stable and making progress. As of spring 2009, 133 of Afghanistan's 356 districts were regarded as high-risk areas, but the rest were labeled as medium or low risk.

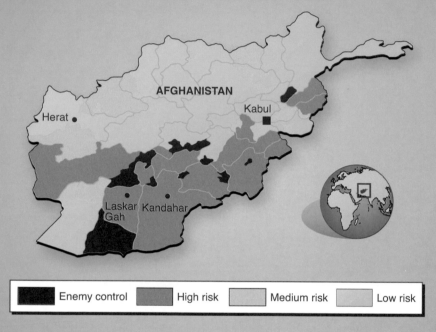

Taken from: Reuters, April 23, 2009.

Afghans benefiting from a small loans scheme which the UK supports are women. . . .

And the people of Afghanistan will next have the opportunity to choose their government in just under four weeks time. The outcome of these elections offers the international community a significant opportunity to better align its shared offer and better articulate the task of the Afghan Government. . . .

Important Economic Growth

Anyone who doubts the importance of this needs only to visit Helmand as I have done this week, where with Governor Mangal's leadership the province has had a record wheat harvest this year, in part because, with funding from my Department, his Food Zone programme has helped persuade 32,000 farmers to plant wheat rather than poppy.[1] . . .

There is a platform on which these initiatives can build. The Afghan economy has grown at up to 10% most years since 2001. And even in 2009, in the midst of the global downturn, growth is projected at 9%. Accelerating growth requires first the maintenance of macroeconomic stability, with advice and support from the IMF [International Monetary Fund] and the World Bank. It also requires policy change to make it easier to start a business and safeguard property rights, together with a sustained effort to build better national and local infrastructure—especially power, water and roads—so that producers can reach markets within and beyond the country's borders.

Finally, progress on each of these vital agenda items will be slowed by fragmentation and accelerated by better co-ordination of the international aid effort. The Afghan National Development Strategy, launched in Paris [in 2008], provides the framework for these efforts. It is natural—and right—that the countries contributing troops to the ISAF [International Security Assistance Force] effort should want to focus part of their effort in the provinces and districts where their soldiers are serving.

In Helmand, along with our immediate stabilisation work backing up our troops, my Department is delivering jobs, infrastructure, health and education services in the province.

EVALUATING THE AUTHORS' ARGUMENTS:

Alexander is a British politician who is knowledgeable about Helmand Province because that area is patrolled by British troops. The author of the following viewpoint, Sandy Shanks, is a novelist, columnist, and a former U.S. Marine. Does knowing the background of these authors influence your opinion of their arguments? In what way? If not, why not?

1. Poppy is used to make the drugs opium and heroin, the sale of which fuels the drug trade and terrorism.

The War in Afghanistan Is a Complete Disaster

Sandy Shanks

> "*I sincerely wish I could impart to readers some good news. We sure could use it in a war that is approaching its ninth year. Alas, there is only bad news.*"

In the following viewpoint Sandy Shanks argues that the war in Afghanistan is not going well. Shanks explains that the United States is the latest in a number of nations and empires that have tried—and failed—to conquer Afghanistan. Since the United States is using pretty much the same tactics as these empires did, Shanks says it can expect to fail there also. Shanks says that as more money and more troops have been poured into the country, the only result has been more death. In Shanks's opinion, the war in Afghanistan is unwinnable because of the country's harsh terrain and the nature of Islamic terrorism: It hails not from any one country, and the terrorists are willing to fight to the death. For all these reasons, Shanks says the war is going badly and the United States can expect to lose it.

Shanks is a columnist and the author of two novels, *The Bode Testament* and *Impeachment*.

A political cartoon said it best. The cartoon depicted a man on the left bemoaning, "Afghanistan is another Vietnam." A bedraggled figure on the right, obviously characterizing an Afghan villager, proclaimed, "Afghanistan is another Afghanistan."

In its past Afghanistan has defeated Alexander the Great, Genghis Khan, various Arab armies, the British Empire, a sundry of other major intruders, as well as the Soviet Union in the eight-year war during the 1980's.

For over 2,500 years Afghanistan has defeated the best and the brightest of the world's empires, earning it the title, "The Graveyard of Empires." On January 13, 1842, a British army doctor reached the British sentry post at Jalalabad, Afghanistan, the lone survivor of a 16,000-strong Anglo-Indian expeditionary force that was massacred in its retreat from Kabul. In the most recent attempt to subdue Afghanistan prior to America's attempts to do so, the [Soviet] Red Army lost 15,000 soldiers. The last should give President [Barack] Obama and his political and military leaders a moment of pause. Obama's attempts to subdue Afghanistan are very similar to the Soviet Union's measures . . . only on a lesser scale. . . .

More Dead, More Wounded, More Blunders

I sincerely wish I could impart to readers some good news. We sure could use it in a war that is approaching its ninth year. Alas, there is only bad news. The July [2009] death toll for Americans was the highest since the war began. Unfortunately, August promises to exceed that heinous record. I understand as a Marine officer [retired] that when one side takes the offensive, that will cause more casualties. But America expects results when we go on the offensive. There are none.

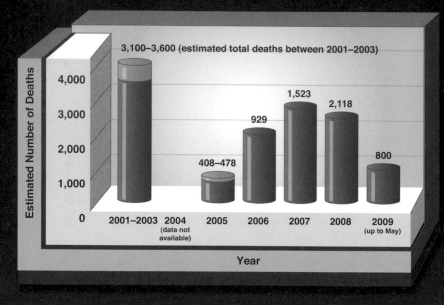

Civilian Deaths in Afghanistan

Remote terrain and poor data collection techniques make it difficult to know for sure how many civilians have died in Afghanistan. But since the start of the war in 2001, at least eight thousand civilians have been killed in the fighting.

Taken from: Human Rights Watch (HRW), United Nations Assistance Mission in Afghanistan (UNAMA), and the British Broadcasting Corporation (BBC).

If there were any positive results of this offensive after more than two months, the Pentagon's public relations branch would be grasping at such news like a drowning sailor reaching out for a lifeline. All we hear is silence. Well, that is not quite true. We are hearing of more dead and wounded American troops. The death of innocent civilians is also on an unprecedented scale.

Chalmers Johnson, a former CIA analyst, is completely unequivocal when it comes to the war in Afghanistan. He boldly proclaims that we are going to lose in Afghanistan.

One of our major strategic blunders in Afghanistan was not to have recognized that both Great Britain and the Soviet Union attempted to pacify Afghanistan using the same military methods as ours and failed disastrously. We seem to have learned nothing from Afghanistan's modern history—to the extent that we even know what it is. Between 1849 and 1947, Britain sent almost annual expeditions against the Pashtun tribes and sub-tribes living in what was then called the North-West Frontier Territories—the area along either side of the artificial border between Afghanistan and Pakistan called the Durand Line.

In addition, Johnson quotes Paul Fitzgerald and Elizabeth Gould, experienced Afghan analysts and coauthors of *Invisible History: Afghanistan's Untold Story.*

If Washington's bureaucrats don't remember the history of the region, the Afghans do. The British used air power to bomb these same Pashtun villages after World War I and were condemned for it. When the Soviets used MiGs [fighter jets] and the dreaded Mi-24 Hind helicopter gunships to do it during the 1980s, they were called criminals. For America to use its overwhelming firepower in the same reckless and indiscriminate manner defies the world's sense of justice and morality while turning the Afghan people and the Islamic world even further against the United States.

Johnson adds, "Our military operations in both Pakistan and Afghanistan have long been plagued by inadequate and inaccurate intelligence about both countries, ideological preconceptions about which parties we should support and which ones we should oppose, and myopic understandings of what we could possibly hope to achieve."

Put a different way, this is not a gunfight. Afghanistan is like fighting in a huge room that contains mirrors within mirrors within mirrors, not unlike a macabre sideshow found at your local county fair. The only difference being the guy shooting at our troops knows where they are. His intelligence is flawless. This is, after all, Pashtun land. . . .

> ## FAST FACT
>
> In October 2009, 53 U.S. troops were killed in Afghanistan—the most in any month since the war began in October 2001.

Sending More Troops to Slaughter

Depending upon your point of view, events seemingly are getting grimmer. General Stanley McChrystal, the newly appointed NATO [North Atlantic Treaty Organization] commander in Afghanistan, is expected to inform President Obama that a further troop surge is needed. Currently, there are 150,000 NATO troops in Afghanistan. He wants to increase that to 300,000. In addition to requesting some 45,000 additional U.S. troops in Afghanistan, the country's top American military commander will ask the Obama administration to double the number of U.S. government civilian workers who are in the country.

In the meantime, politicians in Washington are doing what they do best. In the absence of accomplishments, they issue rhetoric. President Obama [in September 2009] will send Congress a new plan for measuring progress in Afghanistan and Pakistan, in an effort to build confidence among wavering Democrats and to give sharper direction to a costly and increasingly bloody war, White House officials said. A senior administration official who requested anonymity stated, "There's an intense impatience here for results, and I think an absolutely understandable impatience among the American people for results. In the course of August, these plans will be complete." I sure hope that White House insider gets paid a lot of money. By issuing this ludicrous statement to inform Americans, he earned it. That took gall. No wonder the official requested anonymity. . . .

America's Leaders Do Not Get It

There are four concepts America's political and military leadership are not getting.

One, the Islamic extremist fighter is a fanatic. Does the term, "suicide bomber" mean anything to anyone? This fighter would rather die in combat for the glory of Islam than live his squalid life.

Two, the war in Afghanistan is regional, encompassing the entire Middle East, and beyond, notably involving Afghanistan, Iraq, Pakistan, and wherever else this fighter can kill Americans (Yemen, the *Cole*, Oct. 2000)[1] or anyone that is sympathetic to the U.S. This would include Western tourists.

---

1. The author is referring to a 2000 terrorist attack on the USS *Cole*, a military ship that sailed off the coast of Yemen.

U.S. soldiers patrol the Pech Valley in Afghanistan's Kunar Province. Afghanistan's remoteness and rugged terrain make military operations difficult.

Three, Islamic extremists are not represented by any national entity. Defeating the Taliban in Afghanistan in the context of the war against terrorists is a mere myth.

Four, the Islamic extremist wants this regional war to go on and on. How better to kill Americans than in one's own back yard on terrain chosen by the enemy, a major ingredient to victory since the days of the robust Roman Empire.

Islamic extremists, funded by sources in Egypt, Saudi Arabia, Pakistan, Yemen, Syria, Lebanon, etc., want additional troops sent to Afghanistan as U.S. troops in Iraq hunker down in their bases, making them difficult to attack. This plays right into the hands of Islamic extremist groups whose sole objective is to kill American troops sent out by the "Great Satan," Shaytan Al-Akbar in Arabic, referring to America. To these extremists, the Iraq war had its fling, killing over 4,300 Americans and wounding over 35,000. Now it is the turn of Afghanistan, the great "Graveyard of Empires."

As a nation, we have two choices. We either withdraw from the entire Middle East from a ground forces standpoint, or the nation as we known it will die.

Those are our only two choices. Perpetual war is not an option.

EVALUATING THE AUTHOR'S ARGUMENTS:

Sandy Shanks quotes from several sources to support the points he makes in his essay. Make a list of all the people he quotes, including their credentials and the nature of their comments. Then, analyze his sources—are they credible? What makes them qualified to speak on this subject?

Chapter 2

What Challenges Does Afghanistan Face?

An Afghan farmer looks at a government antinarcotics poster. Persuading farmers to give up farming poppies for other cash crops is one of the many challenges the government faces.

Viewpoint

1

The Taliban Threaten Afghanistan and the Rest of the World

"We will continue to play our part in building a secure and democratic Afghanistan because our national security depends on it."

John Hutton

John Hutton is former secretary of state for the British Ministry of Defence. In the following viewpoint he explains why the Taliban are a threat to Afghanistan and to the rest of the world. He reminds readers that the Taliban gave shelter to al Qaeda and allowed them to plot the terrorist attacks of September 11, 2001, which Hutton views as an attack on all of civilization. He also says that the Taliban deprived Afghans of their human rights and used the country as a base for exporting drugs and terrorism. According to Hutton, the Taliban have not been defeated—they continue to hide in Afghanistan and Pakistan, waiting for an opportunity to come back into power. If the world does not act to rid Afghanistan of the Taliban, Hutton warns, they will become more powerful and plot more terrorist attacks. For these reasons, he

John Hutton, "Afghanistan—Worth the Sacrifice (Speech by the Rt Honorable John Hutton, Secretary of State for Defense)," International Institute for Strategic Studies, November 11, 2008.

concludes that winning the war in Afghanistan is vital to the security of Britain and other civilized nations.

AS YOU READ, CONSIDER THE FOLLOWING QUESTIONS:
1. What kind of society does Hutton say the Taliban created when they were in power in Afghanistan?
2. What would have happened if British forces had not gone into southern Afghanistan in 2006, according to Hutton?
3. How many British troops does Hutton say are stationed in Afghanistan?

No politician, whether in government or Parliament, can ever take lightly the decision to commit British forces to military action. In Afghanistan, the deployment of our Armed Forces was in response to an attack on our national interests every bit as unambiguous as the threat presented by the invasion of Belgium in 1914 and the invasion of Poland in 1939 [by the Germans].

A Crime Against All of Civilization

9/11, lest we ever forget, was a crime by Al Qaida against the entire civilised world. It was the largest and most spectacular in a series of attacks from embassies to night clubs, from Kenya to Bali and a worldwide campaign of terror. And they possessed a common thread. Indiscriminate violence. A total disregard for the innocent. For race, nationality, and even religion. It was a strategy designed to provoke disproportionate retaliation. To polarise countries, peoples and religions.

But far from creating division, 9/11 brought the world together, led by the United Nations, to tackle terrorism at its complex and interconnected sources. And as we deal with the cause of those events, we must stay united in purpose against that common threat.

Afghanistan Is at the Heart of the Threat

In 2001, the most important source of the direct threat to the UK and the civilised world was Afghanistan. It was there that 9/11 was planned and facilitated. It was there that Al Qaida had a secure refuge for its franchise of indiscriminate violence.

Afghanistan was Al Qaida's headquarters. From 1996 the Taleban regime gave it sanctuary and assistance, and made 9/11possible.

Let just me remind you what Afghanistan was like then.

The Taleban created a society that was autocratic and despotic. They imposed a religious and social straightjacket on the people. They repressed and killed, with the utmost brutality, to ensure uniformity. They despised knowledge and subjugated women to a brutal and violent existence.

Now these violations of basic human rights might alone be enough to justify action by the international community. But in and of itself, they do not present a national security argument for the deployment of UK forces. This in my mind is a critical distinction. It goes to the heart of the reason why we have 8000 troops in Afghanistan.

An Utterly Repugnant Enemy

We undertook military action in Afghanistan because this was the base from which Al Qaida leaders, through the sanctuary offered by the Taleban, were planning and directing major terrorist operations throughout the world—operations that would, without any doubt at all in my mind, have been aimed at the UK. They were recruiting, indoctrinating and training terrorists. Acting as a communications hub. Generating funding from drugs and other illegal activities.

> **FAST FACT**
>
> The Taliban have claimed responsibility for many deadly bombings, including one in May 2009 in the Pakistani city of Lahore that killed at least thirty-five people.

9/11 didn't then and doesn't now remain the limit of Al Qaida's ambitions. Whilst using Afghanistan as a haven, Al Qaida ran training courses on how to make and use poisons. After 9/11, we found, in Kandahar, a laboratory for developing biological agents, along with evidence that scientists had been recruited to assist in their production. Today, coalition forces are confronted by insurgents whose morality is so depraved that they would use children as human shields and suicide bombers.

Utterly repugnant. But that is what we are up against.

And it is that lethal combination of extremism and willpower that has to be confronted and dealt with.

Afghanistan Is Key to National Security

So, let us be clear: if they had the means no moral compunction would restrain the unleashing of those kinds of destructive forces on the streets of Britain.

Al Qaida and the Taleban had a close and mutually dependent alliance. National security is the primary responsibility of any government. It was and remains in our national security interest to prevent Afghanistan from providing a safe haven for this ruthless terrorist threat. . . .

If we hadn't gone into Southern Afghanistan in 2006 the Taleban would probably now control Southern Helmand and Kandahar. There are many students of history in this room today who would tell us that those who control Kandahar have often controlled Kabul. Which would give free reign to Al Qaida through Afghanistan. Pre 9/11 all over again.

So I am absolutely clear that our commitment to Afghanistan is first and foremost about the UK's national security.

2008 has been a tough year for coalition forces. And, with national elections in 2009, the coming 12 months are likely to be equally as tough. It is going to test the resolve of the international community.

There has been I believe real progress since 2001 but I would be the first to recognise that Afghanistan's system of governance remains fragile; economic growth disappointing; Taleban insurgency in the east and south continues to pose a real challenge; and the dangerous link between terrorism, organised crime and narcotics remains real and obvious.

Now we have set ourselves three strategic objectives. First, that Al Qaida does not return to Afghanistan. Secondly, that Afghanistan remains a legitimate and increasingly effective state, able over time to handle its own security. And thirdly, to prevent the insurgency posing a threat to Afghan peace and prosperity. Achieving these three objectives will define the success of achieving our mission in Afghanistan. . . .

Terrorism Remains a Threat

Now for me, the national security arguments that took us to Afghanistan are stronger today than they were in 2001. If walking away then would have damaged those interests, scuttling away now would deal them a profoundly dangerous blow.

In my view our engagement is as much a security priority for the UK today as the world wars or the cold war of the last century. Terrorism poses a direct threat to the security of the British people. So, let us not for one moment think that it does not threaten our way of life, our values of democracy and human rights.

Now we have experienced the tragic consequences of indiscriminate terrorist action here in our capital city [London]. 52 people died and 700 were injured in a cowardly and shocking act of violence on 7th July 2005. Every week our security and police forces across Britain do an incredible job trying to keep us safe.

Terrorism is a constant threat. One that actually cannot be understated. Wished away or appeased.

Now it has to be confronted. Wherever and whenever it threatens our security here at home. That is why we have 8000 troops in Afghanistan.

We Cannot Withdraw

And to those who say that we can never succeed, that we should walk away and accept defeat, I say simply this: the victims of that kind of defeatism would be the British people. We would have abandoned our ability to tackle terrorism at source. And we would then have to deal with it here on our own streets.

For that is where Al Qaida would eventually manifest itself, escalating the campaign that predated our engagement in Afghanistan. I do not want to see British youngsters being indoctrinated into extremism at new Al Qaida camps ruled by the Taleban in Afghanistan.

Withdrawal would confirm Al Qaida propaganda that Britain, like the Soviet Union before, bombed and then bolted. We would be portrayed as either wrong, callous or weak. And the lesson our friends, vulnerable states, potential aggressors and terrorists would take is that contrary to our experience in the world wars, the Falklands or Northern Ireland, we would give up and go home. Now I believe, very strongly, we must never send such a message. . . .

British defense secretary John Hutton tells a joint session of the House of Commons that the Taliban and al Qaeda continue to pose a threat to Afghanistan and Pakistan.

We will continue to play our part in building a secure and democratic Afghanistan because our national security depends on it. We are making a significant contribution to the coalition's current military effort. Our forces have been heavily committed for several years in both Afghanistan and Iraq. No one can say that the UK is not pulling our weight in the international coalition and we expect others to as well. . . .

Afghanistan Is the Great War of Our Time

The First and Second World Wars were the defining conflicts of the last century. It may be that Afghanistan will be the defining conflict of this century. It does strike to the heart of our interests as a nation. And the preservation of the values that all of us today hold most dear. Timeless values that have been preserved by previous generations. And they continue to define our concepts of right and wrong—good and evil. Democracy. Freedom. Tolerance.

My central argument is that these values are under attack in new ways and by different means today from those which characterised the Two World Wars. But no one should doubt the seriousness of the threat we now face to our freedoms and liberties from those who fight every advance for democracy, every expression of free choice, every manifestation of individual rights.

Now, in taking up this struggle for our own national security, we were right to join the coalition that brought down the Taleban and expelled Al Qaida. We were right to take a lead role in implementing the UN mandate and supporting the democratic Afghan Government. We were right [in 2007] to put our weight behind a comprehensive counter insurgency strategy. And we are right now to commit ourselves to seeing that strategy through.

EVALUATING THE AUTHORS' ARGUMENTS:

John Hutton compares the war in Afghanistan to World War I and World War II. Other authors in this book compare the war in Afghanistan to the Vietnam War. Write three to five sentences on how the war in Afghanistan is similar to both the First and Second World Wars and to the Vietnam War, and then say which war you think the war in Afghanistan has most in common with.

The Taliban Do Not Gravely Threaten Afghanistan or the Rest of the World

John Mueller

"If [the Taliban] came to power again now, they would be highly unlikely to host provocative terrorist groups whose actions could lead to another outside intervention."

In the following viewpoint John Mueller argues that the Taliban do not pose a significant threat to the United States, Afghanistan, or other nations. He says contrary to popular opinion, the Taliban did not play a significant role in the September 11 attacks. Relations between the Taliban and al Qaeda were weak at that point, and evidence shows that the 9/11 attacks were not even plotted from inside Afghanistan. Mueller says the United States overthrew the Taliban in response to 9/11—but the Taliban in fact had nothing to do with the attacks. Furthermore, Mueller says that even if the Taliban came to power again in Afghanistan, they probably would not provide safe haven to any terrorist groups because it would provoke another international war against them. For all these reasons,

John Mueller, "How Dangerous Are the Taliban? Why Afghanistan Is the Wrong War," *Foreign Affairs*, April 15, 2009. Copyright © 2009 by the Council on Foreign Relations, Inc. Reprinted by permission of Foreign Affairs, Inc., www.foreignaffairs.org.

Mueller says it is a mistake to link the Taliban with al Qaeda and the war on terrorism, and he questions whether the war in Afghanistan has any bearing on America's national security.

Mueller is a political science professor at Ohio State University.

AS YOU READ, CONSIDER THE FOLLOWING QUESTIONS:
1. What city and country does Mueller say the September 11 plotters used as their operational base?
2. About how many people are killed by al Qaeda per year outside of war zones, according to Mueller?
3. Who is Glenn Carle, and how does he factor into the author's argument?

George W. Bush led the United States into war in Iraq on the grounds that Saddam Hussein might give his country's nonexistent weapons of mass destruction to terrorists. Now, Bush's successor is perpetuating the war in Afghanistan with comparably dubious arguments about the danger posed by the Taliban and al Qaeda.

President Barack Obama insists [1] that the U.S. mission in Afghanistan is about "making sure that al Qaeda cannot attack the U.S. homeland and U.S. interests and our allies" or "project violence against" American citizens. The reasoning is that if the Taliban win in Afghanistan, al Qaeda will once again be able to set up shop there to carry out its dirty work. As the president puts it [2], Afghanistan would "again be a base for terrorists who want to kill as many of our people as they possibly can."

FAST FACT

According to the America Empire Project, no functioning al Qaeda base camps exist in Afghanistan today.

This argument is constantly repeated but rarely examined; given the costs and risks associated with the Obama administration's plans for the region, it is time such statements be given the scrutiny they deserve.

Multiple sources, including Lawrence Wright's book *The Looming Tower*, make clear that the Taliban was a reluctant host to al Qaeda in the 1990s and felt betrayed when the terrorist group repeatedly violated agreements to refrain from issuing inflammatory statements and fomenting violence abroad. Then the al Qaeda–sponsored 9/11 attacks—which the Taliban had nothing to do with—led to the toppling of the Taliban's regime. Given the Taliban's limited interest in issues outside the "AfPak" region, if they came to power again now, they would be highly unlikely to host provocative terrorist groups whose actions could lead to another outside intervention.

In 2002 FBI director Robert Mueller assured Congress that Afghanistan's Taliban government supported al Qaeda factions in the United States. Subsequent investigations failed to come up with any substantial evidence to support his claims.

And even if al Qaeda were able to relocate to Afghanistan after a Taliban victory there, it would still have to operate under the same siege situation it presently enjoys in what Obama calls its "safe haven" in Pakistan.

The very notion that al Qaeda needs a secure geographic base to carry out its terrorist operations, moreover, is questionable. After all, the operational base for 9/11 was in Hamburg, Germany. Conspiracies involving small numbers of people require communication, money, and planning—but not a major protected base camp.

At present, al Qaeda consists [3] of a few hundred people running around in Pakistan, seeking to avoid detection and helping the Taliban when possible. It also has a disjointed network of fellow travelers around the globe who communicate over the Internet. Over the last decade, the group has almost completely discredited [4] itself in the Muslim world due to the fallout from the 9/11 attacks and subsequent counterproductive terrorism, much of it directed against Muslims. No convincing evidence has been offered publicly to show that al Qaeda Central has put together a single full operation anywhere in the world since 9/11. And, outside of war zones, the violence perpetrated by al Qaeda affiliates, wannabes, and lookalikes combined has resulted [5] in the deaths of some 200 to 300 people per year, and may be declining [6]. That is 200 to 300 too many, of course, but it scarcely suggests that "the safety of people around the world is at stake," as Obama dramatically puts it.

In addition, al Qaeda has yet to establish a significant presence in the United States. In 2002, U.S. intelligence reports asserted that the number of trained al Qaeda operatives in the United States was between 2,000 and 5,000, and FBI Director Robert Mueller assured [7] a Senate committee that al Qaeda had "developed a support infrastructure" in the country and achieved both "the ability and the intent to inflict significant casualties in the U.S. with little warning." However, after years of well funded sleuthing, the FBI and other investigative agencies have been unable [8] to uncover a single true al Qaeda sleeper cell or operative within the country. Mueller's rallying cry has now been reduced [9] to a comparatively bland formulation: "We believe al Qaeda is still seeking to infiltrate operatives into the U.S. from overseas."

Americans Do Not View Afghanistan as a Big Threat

North Korea, Iran, and China all rank as higher threats to national security in the eyes of Americans, according to a 2009 poll.

Which country is a bigger threat to the national security of the United States?

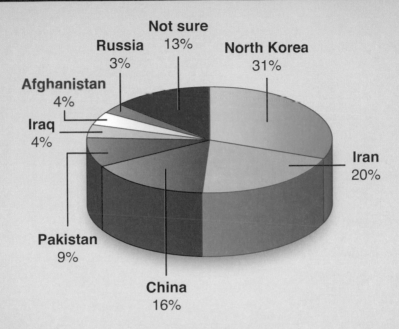

Not sure 13%

Russia 3%

Afghanistan 4%

Iraq 4%

North Korea 31%

Iran 20%

Pakistan 9%

China 16%

Taken from: Rasmussen Reports, August 1–2, 2009.

Even that may not be true. Since 9/11, some two million foreigners have been admitted to the United States legally and many others, of course, have entered illegally. Even if border security has been so effective that 90 percent of al Qaeda's operatives have been turned away or deterred from entering the United States, some should have made it in— —and some of those, it seems reasonable to suggest, would have been picked up by law enforcement by now. The lack of attacks inside the United States combined with the inability of the FBI to find any potential attackers suggests that the

The war in Afghanistan ranked low on the list of most important issues Americans said were facing the country in 2009.

"Which of the following do you see as the most important issue facing the country right now?"

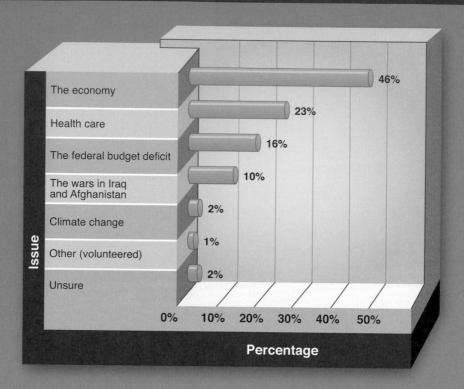

Taken from: Bloomberg poll conducted by Selzer & Co., September, 10–14, 2009.

terrorists are either not trying very hard or are far less clever and capable than usually depicted.

Policymakers and the public at large should keep in mind the words [10] of Glenn Carle, a 23 year veteran of the CIA who served as deputy national intelligence officer for transnational threats: "We must see jihadists for the small, lethal, disjointed and miserable opponents that they are." Al Qaeda "has only a handful of individuals capable of planning, organizing and leading a terrorist operation," Carle notes, and "its capabilities are far inferior to its desires."

President Obama has said that there is also a humanitarian element to the Afghanistan mission. A return of the Taliban, he points out, would condemn the Afghan people "to brutal governance, international isolation, a paralyzed economy, and the denial of basic human rights." This concern is legitimate—the Afghan people appear to be quite strongly opposed to a return of the Taliban, and they are surely entitled to some peace after 30 years of almost continual warfare, much of it imposed on them from outside.

The problem, as Obama is doubtlessly well aware, is that Americans are far less willing to sacrifice lives for missions that are essentially humanitarian than for those that seek to deal with a threat directed at the United States itself. People who embrace the idea of a humanitarian mission will continue to support Obama's policy in Afghanistan—at least if they think it has a chance of success—but many Americans (and Europeans) will increasingly start to question how many lives such a mission is worth.

This questioning, in fact, is well under way. Because of its ties to 9/11, the war in Afghanistan has enjoyed considerably greater public support [11] than the war in Iraq did (or, for that matter, the wars in Korea or Vietnam). However, there has been a considerable dropoff in that support of late. If Obama's national security justification for his war in Afghanistan comes to seem as spurious as Bush's national security justification for his war in Iraq, he, like Bush, will increasingly have only the humanitarian argument to fall back on. And that is likely to be a weak reed.

Links:

[1] http://www.cbsnews.com/stories/2009/03/24/60minutes/main4890687.shtml#ccmm
[2] http://www.nytimes.com/2009/03/27/us/politics/27obama-text.html?_r=1
[3] http://www.newyorker.com/reporting/2008/06/02/080602fa_fact_wright?currentPage=all
[4] http://www.democracyjournal.org/article.php?ID=6622
[5] http://psweb.sbs.ohio-state.edu/faculty/jmueller/ISA2007T.PDF
[6] http://www.humansecuritybrief.info/HSRP_Brief_2007.pdf

[7] http://www.fbi.gov/congress/congress03/mueller021103.htm

[8] http://www.newsweek.com/id/32962

[9] http://www.fbi.gov/congress/congress07/mueller011107.htm

[10] http://www.washingtonpost.com/wp-dyn/content/article/
2008/07/11/AR2008071102710.html

[11] http://www.foreignaffairs.com/articles/61196/john-mueller/the-
iraq-syndrome

**EVALUATING THE AUTHORS'
ARGUMENTS:**

John Mueller contends that if the Taliban were to come to
power in Afghanistan again, they would have little interest in hosting terrorist groups. How do you think John
Hutton, author of the previous viewpoint, would respond
to this argument? With which author do you agree? Name
at least one piece of evidence that swayed you.

Afghanistan Is Not Likely to Become a Democracy

Patrick Basham

"One cannot simply drop a liberal democracy into a country like Afghanistan and expect it to take root."

It is not possible to bring democracy to Afghanistan, argues Patrick Basham in the following viewpoint. Basham says that Afghanistan's tribal, ethnic, and religious groups make it incompatible with democracy. He says that Afghans are more loyal to their tribe, ethnicity, and religion than to their nation. As a result, they will never put their nation first or see their nationality as a common bond. Furthermore, such religious and ethnic loyalties have resulted in strict laws against women and innocent pastimes like music and movies, all of which Basham says are not found in a democratic society. Finally, even though elections have taken place in Afghanistan, these have been corrupt and not at all democratic. For all of these reasons, Basham says that democracy cannot work in Afghanistan the way it does in the United States.

Basham is an adjunct scholar with the Cato Institute, an organization that pro-

Patrick Basham, "Afghanistan's Democratic Debacle," Cato Institute, August 20, 2009. Republished with permission of CATO Institute, conveyed through Copyright Clearance Center, Inc.

motes public policy based on individual liberty, limited government, free markets, and peaceful international relations.

AS YOU READ, CONSIDER THE FOLLOWING QUESTIONS:
1. What corrupt activity does Basham say Hamid Karzai's campaign engaged in during the 2009 Afghan presidential election?
2. What laws does Basham say exist in modern-day Afghanistan that are not compatible with democracy?
3. Who does Basham say are treated like second-class citizens in Afghanistan?

Afghanistan's presidential campaign confirms that Western leaders cannot push Afghan political culture where it doesn't want to go. Today, Afghan democrats could hold a convention in a phone booth.

Although Afghanistan's first presidential (2004) and parliamentary elections (2005) were held in an atmosphere of widespread fear and massive voter intimidation, the international community characterized these elections as watershed moments for Afghan democracy. Events on the ground continue to suggest otherwise. According to the UN, Afghan civilian deaths soared by 24 percent during the first half of 2009. Fears for voter safety on Election Day will shut 10 percent of nearly 7,000 polling stations nationwide.

> **FAST FACT**
>
> More than fifteen different ethnic groups make up the citizenry of Afghanistan. These groups have strong regional, tribal, and religious ties, which has made it historically difficult for them to come together as a nation.

The country's security situation requires 63,000 U.S. troops and 40,500 non-U.S. NATO forces to protect what many consider a rigged election. The UN and the Afghan human rights commission have repeatedly complained about interference in the election by President Hamid Karzai's government.

The most obvious institutional problem is that the election commission is stacked with Karzai's supporters. It's also an open secret that Karzai's campaign has registered three million new voters—swelling the electorate by 17 percent—by allowing males to obtain registration cards for non-existent female relatives.

In Afghan-style elections, campaigning politicians are permitted to broadcast threats against their opponents. On the campaign trail,

Afghan women may have the right to vote, but the Afghan government has passed a law that allows a man to starve his wife to death for refusing to have sex.

moderate presidential candidate Ashraf Ghani, a former finance minister popular with Afghans in America, is literally a marked man whose advertisements are mysteriously destroyed as soon as they appear on billboards.

It's increasingly clear that the Taliban's removal from power did not remove the largest home-grown obstacle to liberal democracy. The Taliban regime represented a 7th century vision of the relationship between religion and the State. They were defeated by those Afghans (allied with the West) with a 12th century vision of man's relationship to his religious and political rulers.

The Diversity of the Afghan People

Afghanistan's citizens identify with many different ethnic groups and speak several different languages. Experts say this is one of the factors that make installing a unified government there difficult.

Afghanistan major ethnic groups

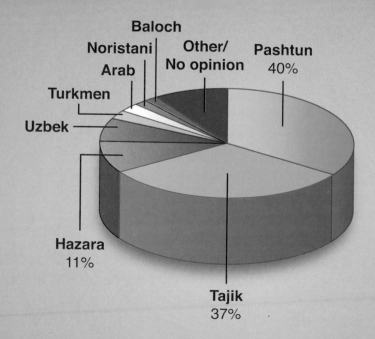

Baloch
Noristani
Arab
Turkmen
Uzbek
Other/No opinion
Pashtun 40%
Hazara 11%
Tajik 37%

Taken from: ABC/BBC poll: December 30, 2008 to January 12, 2009.

Hence, President Karzai is unable to stand up to the Ulema, Afghanistan's conservative religious council, which wields disproportionate political power throughout the country. Cultural traditionalists impose their values by political edict, in the case of Karzai's government, or by force, in the case of the Taliban.

A new law allows a husband to starve his wife if she refuses to have sex, and requires her to get her husband's permission to work. Music shops and other places selling "immoral" goods, such as DVDs, are frequent targets of violence and persecution. The country's culture minister took a private TV network to court to halt its Bollywood soap operas.

But didn't the Afghans in 2004 enact a Western-style constitution that guaranteed political and religious freedom? No, they did not.

The constitution enshrines the country as an Islamic state. While one clause does state that each Afghani citizen is entitled to religious freedom—a portion often highlighted for Western audiences—a far more important passage declares fundamentalist Sharia law to be the supreme law of the land.

American neo-conservatives have spent the past decade proclaiming the universal freedoms that democracies around the world enjoy. The problem is that Afghani political culture doesn't celebrate such freedoms at all. It's an illiberal culture that rewards warlords with political office, requires quotas to ensure female representation in parliament, and tolerates almost indescribably widespread corruption.

President Karzai presides over the fifth most corrupt government in the world, according to a Brookings Institution study. Last year, his government managed to lose a staggering 60 percent of its annual revenue.

What's occurring today in Afghanistan is an affront to supporters of freedom and liberty. But it isn't an affront to most Afghans. For centuries, Afghan politics has been—and will continue to be for the foreseeable future, no matter how many "free" elections are held—about ethnic identity and strict adherence to Islam. Tribal loyalties and religious conservatism trump all other values.

In Kabul's mosques, worshippers hear their clerics robustly support illiberal social policies, including second-class citizenship for women and the persecution of homosexuals. The clerics are saying what a vast majority of Afghanis consider both appropriate and just.

The rhetoric is a vivid reminder that one cannot simply drop a liberal democracy into a country like Afghanistan and expect it to take root. This week's presidential election is the latest demonstration of this stubborn fact.

EVALUATING THE AUTHOR'S ARGUMENTS:

Patrick Basham argues that corruption, mistreatment of women, and strict Islamic and ethnic loyalties make democracy impossible to achieve in Afghanistan. In your opinion, do these constitute insurmountable obstacles to democracy? Why or why not?

Viewpoint

4

Afghanistan Can Become a Democracy

Russell J. Dalton

"Afghans are more positive toward democracy than many of their neighbors, even ranking well compared to democracies such as India and Turkey."

In the following viewpoint Russell J. Dalton reports that the people of Afghanistan hold democracy in very high regard. According to surveys taken of the Afghan people, the vast majority view democracy favorably and associate it with increased rights and liberties rather than just material rewards and a higher standard of living. Dalton says this is promising, for democracy cannot take root in a country whose citizens do not think highly of it. Although many Afghans have little experience with democracy, Dalton says that already existing Afghan institutions—although not perfectly democratic—pave the way for democracy because of their use of collective decision-making skills. Dalton concludes that the high regard in which democracy is held in Afghanistan makes it possible to believe it can have a promising future there.

Dalton is a political science professor and former director of the Center for the Study of Democracy at the University of California at Irvine.

Russell J. Dalton, "The Road to Democracy in Afghanistan," *Statebuilding, Security, and Social Change in Afghanistan: Reflections on a Survey of the Afghan People,* June 30, 2008, pp. 67, 70–75. Copyright © 2008 The Asia Foundation. Reproduced by permission of the author.

AS YOU READ, CONSIDER THE FOLLOWING QUESTIONS:

1. What percent of Afghans agree with the statement, "Democracy is better than any other form of government"?
2. What rights do 83 percent of Afghans associate with democracy, as reported by Dalton?
3. What percent of Afghans does Dalton say link democracy to peace and stability? How does this number compare to other transitional nations?

An important long-term element in any democratic transition is the development of public support for the democratic ideal that will sustain the new political process. It is difficult for any democracy to endure if the citizenry does not value and understand the democratic process. While the Afghan state and its political systems are struggling to develop a functional system of democratic government, this report asks how ordinary citizens view democracy, and their understanding of this concept.

Afghans Are Supportive of Democracy

The 2008 survey asked Afghans whether they agree or disagree with the Churchillian statement: "Democracy may have its problems, but it is better than any other form of government". A full 78 percent of Afghans agree with this statement, which is a positive sign of their democratic aspirations. This is slightly below the 84 percent in 2006 and 85 percent in 2007 that endorsed democracy in this question. Compared to other nations in the region, however, Afghans are more positive toward democracy than many of their neighbors, even ranking well compared to democracies such as India and Turkey. Given Afghanistan's modern political history, this high level of democratic support is striking.

Afghan Institutions Can Form the Basis of Democracy

The previous description of public support for democracy makes presumptions about how Afghans understand the term "democracy." Given the nation's political history and socio-economic condition one might reasonably wonder about the content of these opinions. The majority of the Afghan adult public has never attended school, lives in a rural area, and has limited access to electricity or modern information sources. These are not ideal conditions for understanding the meaning of democracy. Indeed, one often hears claims that support for democracy in developing nations lacks meaning because it reflects a desire for the higher standard of living in established democracies rather than support for basic democratic rights and principles.

At the same time, in 2008 Afghanistan has already held multiple democratic elections with extensive efforts at civic education during pre-electoral periods and additional democracy-building efforts by the government and international organizations. Hundreds of

Afghan election workers check suspicious ballots during a recount of the August 20, 2009, presidential election. Seventy-eight percent of Afghans support democracy even though political fraud is widespread.

international and Afghan NGOs [nongovernmental organizations] have been active in educating the public about democratic processes and principles and developing the basis of a meaningful civil society. Furthermore, Afghans' understanding of democracy could draw upon elements of civic governance in the nation's history, such as the *jirga* tradition, representative bodies like *shura* and the legacy of the 1964 constitution. Even though these traditional institutions fall short of the democratic ideal, most notably in their traditional exclusion of women, they provide an example of deliberation and collective decision-making that can provide a basis for expanding participation and democratic practices. Indirect evidence of how the experience of traditional governance mechanisms can positively inform attitudes towards democracy is provided elsewhere in the survey which shows greater support for democracy among those who are positive toward their community jirga and shura. . . .

FAST FACT

A 2009 ABC News/BBC/ARD poll asked Afghans whether they think of themselves more as Afghans or as members of their ethnic group—72 percent said they are Afghans first, causing some to hope that democracy will soon thrive in the nation.

Afghans Are Gaining Experience with Democracy

The most direct way to assess public understanding of democracy is to simply ask people what the term means to them. The Asia Foundation has regularly monitored public understanding of democracy, beginning with a 2004 Voter Education Survey. In the lead-up to the 2004 elections many Afghans were still uncertain about democracy and the democratic process. For instance, many were unfamiliar with the process of free and fair elections because these were unknown to them. Yet, already in 2004, almost half of Afghans defined democracy in terms of some variant of liberal political rights, which is fairly high in comparison to other newly democratizing nations.

Experience with democracy and public education programs have increased the proportion expressing an opinion since 2004. Most people give multiple definitions of democracy. The primary definition of democracy includes a set of liberal political rights—freedom, rights and law, women's rights, and government by the people. Such rights are mentioned by the vast majority of respondents (83%). Attention to liberal political rights is higher in Afghanistan than in most other

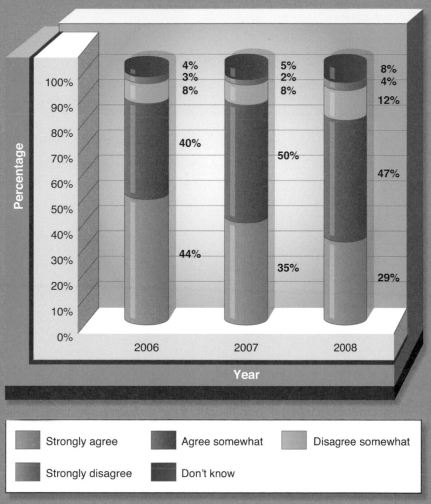

Afghans Support Democracy

The majority of Afghans say that democracy is better than other forms of government.

Legend:
- Strongly agree
- Agree somewhat
- Disagree somewhat
- Strongly disagree
- Don't know

Taken from: 2006, 2007, and 2008 Asia Foundation surveys.

Afghans understand democracy to include a number of important rights and liberties, rather than just material gains.

	Meaning of Democracy (%)*			Benefits of Democracy (%)*		
	2004	2006	2008	2004	2006	2008
Don't Know/Nothing	36	4	9	37	4	21
Political Rights	54	84	83	50	85	67
Freedom	39	55	53	30	37	33
Rights and law	21	31	23	24	33	19
Government by the people	20	33	22	14	29	19
Women's rights	11	20	17	16	23	16
Elections	4	14	11	5	14	9
Peace, Stability, Security	20	38	34	27	42	35
Economic Gains, Prosperity	8	17	16	16	22	16
Other Political Options	9	25	24	12	32	48
Islamic democracy	8	23	20	11	31	19
Communism	1	2	3	1	1	1
Better government/less corruption	–	–	–	–	–	34

*Percentages total to more than 100 percent because multiple responses were possible.

Taken from: 2004, 2006, and 2008 Asia Foundation surveys.

transitional systems, implying that these rights have a special value to the Afghan public. This is a positive sign that citizen education efforts and experience have deepened public understanding of democracy. Moreover, as the number of political rights cited by an individual increases, so too does their belief that democracy is better than other forms of government. Among those who do not cite any political rights in defining democracy, only 18 percent strongly approve of democracy as a form of government, but this increases to 42 percent among those who cite three or more political rights.

Afghans Link Democracy with Greater Rights and Freedoms

Democracy building efforts often focus on elections, but elections are mentioned by only 11 percent of respondents. This implies that

Afghans see democracy not just as a set of processes and institutions, but as a means to provide rights, liberty and freedom. The percentage of Afghans who link democracy to peace and stability (34%) is higher than in most transitional societies, reflecting Afghanistan's violent modern history and the continuing conflict in the nation. A smaller percentage identify democracy with economic prosperity (16%). Both of these responses have actually decreased since 2006 and remain secondary meanings of democracy. This is also a positive sign, because it suggests that Afghans do not define democracy primary in terms of improving their immediate situation, but in terms of broader rights and liberties. . . .

Support for democracy as an ideal is important in building a democratic political culture, but such a culture should also include understanding and support for the substantive values that underlie the democratic process. Since 2004 The Asia Foundation surveys have asked about support for several basic democratic values. Already in 2004 there was nearly universal support for the principle of equal rights regardless of gender, ethnicity or religion. These sentiments have dipped slightly since 2006, but remain close to the 2004 levels. Similarly, there is widespread support for allowing peaceful political opposition, which is also relatively stable over time. Other items in the survey demonstrate continued support for gender equality by most Afghans which is another strikingly positive indicator of democratic rights. . . .

Democracy Has a Hopeful Future in Afghanistan

Certainly, one must be cautious in interpreting these findings. The majority of the public is still learning about the democratic process and is unlikely to understand the full benefits and limitations of a democratic system. The development of a deeply felt democratic political culture is a process that takes decades, not just a few years. Society must also change to reflect democratic values. Similarly, it is not realistic to think that when Afghans express support for democracy this carries the same meaning as when citizens say the same in established democracies because the latter have a long history of democratic experiences that underlie their views.

Yet, expressed support for democracy does exist among the Afghan public, and this is much better than the opposite. These newly formed aspirations can erode, however, if the democratic process does not successfully address the nation's problems and needs of communities. Some erosion is apparent since 2006–07, but changes so far have been at the margins. Most Afghans have experienced the autocratic alternatives to democracy, and believe democracy is better than these other forms of government. However, performance is not meeting their expectations, and improvements are necessary to deepen the public's commitment to democracy.

EVALUATING THE AUTHOR'S ARGUMENTS:

Russell J. Dalton uses history and statistics to make his point that democracy is possible in Afghanistan. He does not, however, use any quotations to support his arguments. If you were to rewrite this viewpoint and insert quotations, what authorities might you quote from? Where would you place these quotations to bolster the points Dalton makes?

Women Must Be Respected If Democracy Is to Succeed in Afghanistan

Yifat Susskind

"There can be no democracy in a place where half the population is considered the property of the other half."

In the following viewpoint Yifat Susskind details the ways in which women's rights are threatened in Afghanistan. Women are completely marginalized in Afghan society, she says—they are routinely threatened, murdered, and mistreated. Susskind says that true democracy cannot exist in a country where half the population is treated so poorly and fails to be represented by the government. She urges both the Afghan and U.S. governments to make women's rights a greater priority if they want to see democracy flourish in Afghanistan.

Yifat Susskind is the policy and communications director for the women's rights organization MADRE. Her articles have appeared in TomPaine.com, *Foreign Policy in Focus*, AlterNet, and *Z Magazine*.

AS YOU READ, CONSIDER THE FOLLOWING QUESTIONS:
1. Who is Sitara Achakzai, and how does she factor into the author's argument?
2. What antidemocratic law does Susskind say President Hamid Karzai signed into law in April 2009?
3. How is the United States guilty of betraying Afghan women's rights, according to the author?

By the time the first ballot is cast in Afghanistan's August 20 [2009] election, hopes for a democratic outcome will already be dead. The [Barack] Obama Administration is billing Afghanistan's second Parliamentary election in 30 years as a milestone in that country's march towards democracy. But there can be no democracy in a place where half the population is considered the property of the other half. That's why some of Afghanistan's toughest, most tenacious pro-democracy activists are women. They understand that democracy is more than a procedural election; women's rights and genuine democracy are interdependent.

The Murder of Afghan Women

A July United Nations report about violence against women in Afghanistan grimly confirms what women there have been telling us all year: public assassinations of women are on the rise. Most at risk are those who dare to hold jobs, speak out for their rights, send their daughters to school, or simply appear in public without a male chaperone. The killings are inherently political, aimed at creating a society in which women have no rights and no role in public life.

On April 12, 2009, Sitara Achakzai was gunned down in front of her home. The motive was clear. As an elected leader in Kandahar's provincial council, she used that position to fight for women's human rights. Just the previous month, she helped organize a national sit-in of thousands of women for International Women's Day. Fundamentalists took her life to send a message: that women have no right to speak out, to act and to be heard.

The Government Is Not Committed to Women's Rights

The Taliban has claimed responsibility for the killings of numerous other women this year. We don't know exactly how many because the government isn't keeping track. That's precisely the problem, say many women's rights activists: government inaction amounts to complicity. Any policy wonk can tell you that without the data to illustrate a social problem, you can't push for a policy remedy. And a remedy is what governments are supposed to provide when their citizens are being hunted down and killed for exercising basic human rights.

Even President [Hamid] Karzai, whom the US hand-picked in 2001 to lead the new, "democratic" Afghanistan, has displayed no real commitment to women's rights. In April [2009], he signed a law that allows marital rape and forces women to ask their husbands' permission to leave the house. The law was revised only after Afghan women risked their lives to wage street protests in Kabul, generating an international outcry that Karzai could not ignore.

When pressed, Karzai admitted that he hadn't actually read the bill before signing it. Clearly, his concern was not for the women who would be bound by the reactionary law, but for the ultra-conservative proponents of the law who can make or break him in this election. That's always been the status of women's rights in Afghan politics: a mere bargaining chip. Just as young girls are traded to resolve disputes between families, women's rights are traded between leaders hashing out what Afghan society should look like.

Women's Rights Have Been Traded

The US, too, is guilty of horse-trading in Afghan women's rights. From 2001 to 2005, the most powerful man in Afghanistan was US Special Envoy and then Ambassador, Zalmay Khalilzad. His approach to Afghanistan's fundamentalists and warlords was sheer appeasement, which he prefers to call "cooperation through cooptation."

It was Khalilzad who made sure that brutal militia leaders, including war criminals, were appointed as cabinet ministers, judges and regional governors after Afghanistan's first US-sponsored election in 2004, and that the country's new Constitution tethered Afghans to arbitrary and reactionary interpretations of Islam.

The April 12, 2009, murder of legislator Sitara Achakzai by Taliban sympathizers has highlighted the increasing violence against supporters of women's rights in Afghanistan.

Like their counterparts in all religions, Afghanistan's fundamentalists wanted state institutions that would ensure the subordination of women. What Khalilzad wanted in return was enough stability in Afghanistan to pursue the Bush-era goal of permanent US global dominance. Women's rights—and with them Afghanistan's prospects for real democracy—were apparently an easy trade for him to make.

There Cannot Be Democracy Without Women's Rights

The result was a government riddled with warlords whose track record on women's rights is hardly better than the Taliban's. In 2003, when 25-year-old MP [member of parliament] Malalai Joya stepped up to the microphone and accused her warlord colleagues of committing atrocities and oppressing women, they physically attacked her and threatened to rape her. She has since survived four assassination attempts.

Other defenders of women's rights have not been so lucky. Malalai Kakar rose through the ranks to become a leading police officer in her province, focusing on crimes against women. Safia Amajan devoted her life to teaching and promoting girls' education. In June, a midwife named Narges, who was the only health worker in the community, was murdered along with her husband and seven-year-old son. All of these women were brutally killed for the very acts that made them inspirations.

These women are all part of the beleaguered but vibrant Afghan women's movement that confronts both US air strikes and Taliban death threats to secure food, housing, healthcare and education for women and their families, defend women's shelters, hold peace demonstrations, demand women's full participation in public life and fight for interpretations of Islam that support women's rights. No foreign military occupation is going to do this. The US may be able to produce an election in Afghanistan on August 20, but it can't produce a society based on human rights. It's the women of Afghanistan who will secure their own rights and enable genuine democracy in the process.

EVALUATING THE AUTHORS' ARGUMENTS:

Susskind explains why she thinks the U.S.-backed August 2009 elections in Afghanistan did not represent a democratic achievement for that nation. After considering her arguments, do you agree with her? Or, do you agree with other authors in this chapter who argue that democracy must take small steps to succeed in Afghanistan? Explain.

Viewpoint 6

Afghanistan Suffers from Corrupt Elections

Malalai Joya

"Rather than democracy, what we have in Afghanistan today are back room deals amongst discredited warlords."

In the following viewpoint Malalai Joya argues that Afghanistan's elections are tainted by fraud and corruption. Although the West—and particularly the United States—has touted the elections as a sign that democracy has come to Afghanistan, Joya says in reality it has not. In her opinion, the candidates are all either criminals, conspirators, or men who are willing to trade the rights of Afghan women for money and power. Joya says that some of the candidates are the very warlords who have kept Afghanistan undemocratic for years. She calls the Afghan elections a facade of democracy and urges the United States to demand real democratic change in that nation.

Joya is an Afghan citizen. In 2005 she was the youngest person ever to be elected to the Afghan parliament. She is the author of the book *A Woman Among Warlords.*

Like millions of Afghans, I have no hope in the results of this week's [August 2009] election. In a country ruled by warlords, occupation forces, Taliban insurgency, drug money and guns, no one can expect a legitimate or fair vote.

Criminals for Candidates

Among the people on the street, a common sentiment is, "Everything has already been decided by the U.S. and NATO [North Atlantic Treaty Organization], and the real winner has already been picked by the White House and Pentagon." Although there are a total of 41 candidates running for president, the vast majority of them are well known faces responsible for the current disastrous situation in Afghanistan.

Hamid Karzai has cemented alliances with brutal warlords and fundamentalists in order to maintain his position. Although our Constitution forbids war criminals from running for office, he has named two notorious militia commanders as his vice-presidential running mates—Qasim Fahim, who was, at the time of the 2001 invasion, the warlord who headed up the Northern Alliance, and Karim Khalili. The election commission did not reject them or a number of others accused of many crimes, and so the list of candidates also includes former Russian puppets and a former Taliban commander.

> **FAST FACT**
>
> According to Peter W. Galbraith, a former United Nations representative in Afghanistan, one in three votes cast in the August 2009 presidential elections in that country were fraudulent.

Rashid Dostum, former exiled warlord turned Afghan presidential candidate, speaks to supporters at a rally. Karzai's government has made deals with Dostum in return for his support during the election.

Deals Rather than Democracy

Karzai has also continued to absolutely betray the women of Afghanistan. Even after massive international outcry and brave protesters taking to the streets of Kabul, Karzai has implemented the infamous law targeting Shia [a Muslim sect] women. He had initially promised to review the most egregious clauses, but in the end it was passed with few amendments, leaving the barbaric anti-women statements untouched. As Human Rights Watch recently said, "Karzai has made an unthinkable deal to sell Afghan women out in return for the support of fundamentalists in the August 20 election."

Deals have been made with countless fundamentalists in Karzai's maneuvering to stay in power. For example, pro-Iranian extremist Haji Mohammad Mohaqiq, who has been accused of war crimes, has been promised five cabinet positions for his party, and so he has told the media he's backing Karzai. A deal has even been done with the dreaded warlord Rashid Dostum—who has returned from exile in Turkey to campaign for Karzai—and many other such terrorists.

Rather than democracy, what we have in Afghanistan today are back room deals amongst discredited warlords.

No Real Choice Among Candidates

The two main contenders to Karzai's continued rule, Ashraf Ghani Ahmadzai and Abdullah Abdullah, do not offer any change; both are former cabinet ministers in this discredited regime and neither has a real, broad footing amongst the people.

Abdullah has run a high profile campaign, in part due to the backing and financial support he receives from Iran's fundamentalist regime. Abdullah and some of the Northern Alliance commanders supporting him have threatened unrest if he loses the vote, raising fears of a return to the rampant violence and killing that marked the civil war years of 1992 to 1996. All of the major candidates' speeches and policies are very similar. They make the same sweet-sounding promises, but we are not fooled. Afghans remember how Karzai abandoned his campaign pledges after winning the 2004 vote.

Afghan Elections Are for Show

We Afghans know that this election will change nothing and it is only part of a show of democracy put on by and for the West, to legitimize

Corruption Is a Major Problem in Afghanistan

More than three-quarters of Afghans said that corruption is a major problem in their country.

Corruption in . . .	Major problem %	Minor problem %	Not a problem %
Daily life	51	29	18
Neighborhood	48	35	14
Local authorities	53	33	10
Provincial government	63	26	7
In Afghanistan as a whole	76	16	4

Taken from: 2008 Asia Foundation survey.

its future puppet in Afghanistan. It seems we are doomed to see the continuation of this failed, mafia-like corrupt government for another term.

The people of Afghanistan are fed up with the rampant corruption of Karzai's "narco-state" government—his own brother, Wali Karzai, has been linked to drug trafficking in Kandahar Province—and the escalating war waged by NATO. In May of [2009], U.S. air strikes killed approximately 150 civilians in my native province, Farah. More than ever, Afghans are faced with powerful internal enemies—fundamentalist warlords and their Taliban brothers-in-creed—and the external enemies occupying the country.

Democracy will never come to Afghanistan through the barrel of a gun, or from the cluster bombs dropped by foreign forces. The struggle will be long and difficult, but the values of real democracy, human rights and women's rights will only be won by the Afghan people themselves.

The West Must Push for Real Democracy in Afghanistan

So do not be fooled by this façade of democracy. Your governments in the West that claim to be bringing democracy to Afghanistan ignore public opinion in their own countries, where growing numbers are against the war. President [Barack] Obama in particular needs to understand that the change Afghans believe in does not include more troops and a ramped up war.

If the populations of Afghanistan and the NATO countries were able to vote on this military occupation it could not continue indefinitely, and peace would finally be within reach.

EVALUATING THE AUTHORS' ARGUMENTS:

The author of this viewpoint, Malalai Joya, is a former Afghan politician. The author of the following viewpoint, Gary Hart, is a former American politician. In what way do these authors' backgrounds influence your opinion of their argument? Are you more likely to believe one over the other? Why or why not?

Afghanistan's Elections Are a Sign of Progress

Gary Hart

> *"For the smaller group of us who saw the glass half full, [the Afghan national election] was an inspiring experience."*

People should not be so critical or skeptical of the 2009 Afghan elections, argues Gary Hart in the following viewpoint. He says he is disappointed by people who have criticized the elections as being plagued by violence or not representative of true democracy. Hart says the Afghan voters are very brave—they endured threatening conditions and voted in numbers that rivaled voter turnout even in the United States. Hart says the Afghan elections are even more impressive when one considers that they featured many female candidates—and yet just a few years ago, the Taliban were executing women en masse just miles from where the U.S. embassy now stands. He concludes that although democracy in Afghanistan has a long way to go, the August 2009 elections represented an important democratic milestone for the Afghan people.

Hart served as a U.S. senator from Colorado from 1975–1987. He was a

Gary Hart, "In Afghanistan, the True Meaning of Democracy," *Denver Post,* August 25, 2009, Guest Commentary. Reproduced by permission of the author.

member of the National Democratic Institute senior election observer group for the August 2009 Afghanistan national election.

AS YOU READ, CONSIDER THE FOLLOWING QUESTIONS:
1. What does Hart say was different about the 2009 and 2004 Afghan elections?
2. What conditions does Hart say Afghan citizens endured so they could vote?
3. Who is Nurzia, and how does she factor into Hart's argument?

"We believe that our government is weak, stupid, overbearing, dishonest, and inefficient, and also believe it to be the best in the world and would like to offer it to others." This insight of Professor Michael Kammen came to mind as I drove around the teeming, dusty streets of Kabul [in August 2009].

The Afghan Struggle for Democracy

The United States has an enormous military, political and economic presence in Afghanistan, which will increase before it decreases, trying to bring to the Afghan people the kind of government against which Americans have been screaming in so-called town hall meetings recently. Many Afghanis are dying and risking their lives to achieve even a semblance of the kind of government many Americans seem to distrust at best and hate at worst.

Perhaps it is because this ancient culture is tired and wishes a halt to everyone using it as a modern-day version of the OK Corral for the U.S. Army and the Taliban.

Unlike Iraq, however, we didn't send our Army there because we wanted to; we did so because our

> **FAST FACT**
>
> In the days leading up to the August 2009 elections in Afghanistan, more than forty terrorist attacks occurred across the country. Despite this, at least 5,662,758 voters—or 38 percent of Afghan citizens—turned out to vote, according to the Independent Election Commission of Afghanistan.

most recent day of infamy, 9/11, originated there. And, partly because we chose not to finish the job in 2002, we are now back to pick up where we left off seven years ago.

As a member of a small international group observing the second presidential election in this very old country's history, these reflections are rendered not to stimulate debate about American policy in Afghanistan but to reflect on 21st century democracy and what it means through a different set of eyes and, strangely enough, to ponder whether the Afghan people, even in their desperate life-and-death struggle, might have a lesson for us.

The Afghan Elections Were Inspirational

A small army of media, non-governmental organizations, and members of the international community blanketed [the August 2009] election focusing on the same questions that dominate U.S. elections:

Despite Taliban threats of violence, Afghan women line up to vote in the August 2009 presidential election. Some believe the election was a sign of gradual progress to true democracy.

winners and losers; voter turnout; rumors of manipulation and fraud; and, in this case, numbers of dead and wounded. Within 48 hours, most of this army was at the airport, headed for the next war zone or arena of excitement.

The skeptics concluded that the turnout was low, especially in the hostile south and east, too many women stayed away out of fear, and as many as 50 or more were killed on election day. For the smaller group of us who saw the glass half full, however, it was an inspiring experience. Despite ancient cultural and religious traditions of misogyny, a surprising number of candidates of provincial councils were women, and women voted in appreciable numbers in the safer regions. Unlike the only previous national presidential election in 2004, this election was managed by the Afghan government and included an independent election commission. The candidates spoke to issues of great public concern and avoided attacks and acrimony much more, it must be said, than in American elections. No one called any of the candidates "socialists" or "communists."

Do Not Be Skeptical About the Afghan Elections

Though we do not know for certain yet, the turnout could be in the range of 40 percent of eligible voters. This was considered a setback, even a failure, by some media analysts. Asked my opinion at a press conference on Saturday, I stated this: "I do not know of one mature democracy, including my own, where, faced with the threat of death for voting, the turnout would be 40 percent."

Against incredible odds, the Afghan people showed amazing courage, fortitude and determination. They are to be respected, admired and honored. Many stood in lines, amidst heat and dust, for considerable periods of time, exposed not just to the elements, but to potential rocket-propelled grenades, car bombs, and drive-by assassins. Only a few years before, in a soccer stadium not far from the U.S. Embassy, 30,000 people or more filled the seats to watch masked Taliban thugs force women to their knees and shoot them in the back of the head.

We Should Respect the Bravery of Afghan Voters

Last Thursday, a woman called Nurzia, the mother of four, took her children with her to vote. Like many others, she was asked if she was afraid. "Why should we be afraid?" she said. "We came to have a say in our future and for our children."

It is left to us to ponder whether any of us has her courage or her understanding of what genuine democracy truly means.

EVALUATING THE AUTHOR'S ARGUMENTS:

Hart says that Afghans are fighting and dying to establish the kind of democratic government that Americans take for granted. Do you agree with him? Do you think that Americans take their democracy for granted? Or is their criticism of their government actually a sign of democracy at work?

Chapter 3

How Should the United States Proceed in Afghanistan?

The United States faces critical decisions on troop levels and general strategy to end the war in Afghanistan.

The United States Should Leave Afghanistan

Ralph Peters

"Instead of floundering in search of a strategy, we should consider removing the bulk, if not all, of our forces."

In the following viewpoint Ralph Peters argues that the United States needs to get out of Afghanistan. He says the war has gone badly and has no hope of succeeding because Afghanistan is not able to be turned into a modern country. Its remote landscape, coupled with its feudal history, makes it impossible to adopt any kind of working rule of law, says Peters. In his opinion, the United States should never have attempted to turn Afghanistan into a modern state—after September 11, it should have smashed the Taliban and then left. Peters says pouring more troops, money, and resources into the country will only result in bankruptcy and death. For all of these reasons, he advises the United States to cut its losses and get out of Afghanistan before it gets mired there for decades.

Peters is a retired army officer and the author of *Looking for Trouble: Adventures in a Broken World.*

AS YOU READ, CONSIDER THE FOLLOWING QUESTIONS:
1. What, according to Peters, was America's "great mistake" in Afghanistan?
2. What does Peters say would be the best option for the United States to pursue in Afghanistan?
3. What does Peters say would be the worst option for the United States to pursue in Afghanistan?

The conflict in Afghanistan is the wrong war in the wrong place at the wrong time. Instead of concentrating on the critical mission of keeping Islamist terrorists on the defensive, we've mired ourselves by attempting to modernize a society that doesn't want to be—and cannot be—transformed.

Blind to the Growing Crisis

In the absence of a strategy, we're doubling our troop commitment, hoping to repeat the success we achieved in the profoundly different environment of Iraq. Unable to describe our ultimate goals with any clarity, we're substituting means for ends.

Expending blood and treasure blindly in Afghanistan, we do our best to shut our eyes to the worsening crisis next door in Pakistan, a radicalizing Muslim state with more than five times the population and a nuclear arsenal. We've turned the hose on the doghouse while letting the mansion burn.

Our Fatal Mistake

Initially, Afghanistan wasn't a war of choice. We had to dislodge and decimate al-Qaeda, while punishing the Taliban and strengthening friendlier forces in the country. Our great mistake was to stay on in an attempt to build a modernized rule-of-law state in a feudal realm with no common identity.

We needed to smash our enemies and leave. Had it proved necessary, we could have returned later for another punitive mission. Instead, we fell into the great American fallacy of believing ourselves responsible for helping those who've harmed us. This practice was already fodder for mockery 50 years ago, when the novella and film *The Mouse That Roared* postulated that the best way for a poor country to get rich was to declare war on America then surrender.

Even if we achieved the impossible dream of creating a functioning, unified state in Afghanistan, it would have little effect on the layered crises in the Muslim world. Backward and isolated, Afghanistan is sui generis [only example of its kind]. Political polarization in the U.S. precludes an honest assessment, but Iraq's the prize from which positive change might flow, while Afghanistan could never inspire neighbors who despise its backwardness.

Critics say that Afghan president Hamid Karzai puts his own self-interest above that of his countrymen and gives in to the Taliban too readily.

Pouring In Resources with No Return

Echoing Vietnam, we're pouring wealth into Afghanistan, corrupting those we wish to rally; we're fighting with restrictions against an enemy who enjoys sanctuaries across international borders; and our core enemies are natives, not foreign parties (as al-Qaeda was in Iraq).

FAST FACT

More than $228.2 billion was spent on U.S. combat operations in Afghanistan between 2002 and 2009.

If the impending surge fails to pacify the country, will we send another increment of troops, then another, as we did in Southeast Asia? As the British learned the hard way, Afghanistan can be disciplined, but it can't be profitably occupied or liberalized. It's inconceivable to us, but many Afghans prefer their lives to the lives we envision for them. The lot of women is hideous, and the lives of nearly all the people are nasty, brutish and short. But the culture is theirs.

Even "our man in Kabul," President Hamid Karzai, put his self-interest above any greater cause. Reborn a populist, he backs every Taliban claim that the U.S. inflicts only civilian casualties in virtually every effort against terrorists. Karzai is convinced that we can't abandon him.

The United States Needs to Leave Afghanistan

We should do just that. Instead of floundering in search of a strategy, we should consider removing the bulk, if not all, of our forces. The alternative is to hope blindly, waste more lives and resources, and, in the worst case, see our vulnerable supply route through Pakistan cut, forcing upon our troops the most ignominious retreat since Korea in 1950 (a massive air evacuation this time around, leaving a wealth of military gear).

Ranked from best to worst, here are our four basic options going forward:

- Best. Instead of increasing the U.S. military "footprint," reduce our forces and those of NATO [North Atlantic Treaty Organization] by two-thirds, maintaining a "mother ship" at Bagram Air Base and a few satellite bases from which special operations troops, aircraft and drones, and lean conventional forces would strike terrorists and support Afghan factions with whom we share common enemies. All resupply for our military could be done by air, if necessary.

Stop pretending Afghanistan's a real state. Freeze development efforts. Ignore the opium. Kill the fanatics.

- Good. Leave entirely. Strike terrorist targets from over the horizon and launch punitive raids when necessary. Instead of facing another Vietnam ourselves, let Afghanistan become a Vietnam

Afghans Are Growing Weary of War

Since 2005, support for the United States, the direction of Afghanistan as a nation, Afghan president Hamid Karzai, and of the international coalition has dropped sharply among the people of Afghanistan.

Afghans with a positive view of the following:

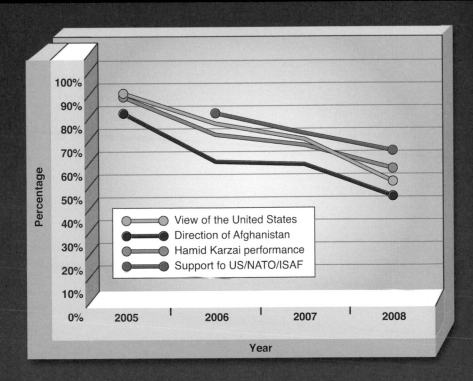

Taken from: ABC/BBC poll: December 30, 2008 to January 12, 2009.

for Iran and Pakistan. Rebuild our military at home, renewing our strategic capabilities.

- Poor. Continue to muddle through as is, accepting that achieving any meaningful change in Afghanistan is a generational commitment. Surge troops for specific missions, but not permanently.
- Worst. Augment our forces endlessly and increase aid in the absence of a strategy. Lie to ourselves that good things might just happen. Let U.S. troops and Afghans continue to die for empty rhetoric, while Pakistan decays into a vast terrorist refuge.

A Reality Check Is Needed

In any event, Pakistan, not Afghanistan, will determine the future of Islamist extremism in the region. And Pakistan is nearly lost to us—a fact we must accept. Our strategic future lies with India.

President [Barack] Obama pitched Afghanistan as the good war during his campaign, while rejecting our efforts in Iraq as a sideshow. He got it exactly wrong. Now our new president either needs to lay out a coherent, detailed strategy with realistic goals, or accept that, by mid-2002, we had achieved all that conventional forces could manage in Afghanistan.

We don't need hope. We need the audacity of realism.

EVALUATING THE AUTHOR'S ARGUMENTS:

Peters says the United States was wrong to think it could change the lives or culture of the Afghan people. In two or three sentences, explain what he means by this. Then, state whether you agree. Do you think the United States should try to change cultures that are different from its own? Why or why not?

The United States Should Not Leave Afghanistan

Marie Cocco

"We have forgotten that the terrorist attacks of Sept. 11, 2001, demanded that we go to war in Afghanistan."

The United States must stay in Afghanistan, argues Marie Cocco in the following viewpoint. She reminds Americans why they are fighting there in the first place—because on September 11, 2001, America was attacked by terrorists who used Afghanistan as a training base. She thinks Americans have forgotten this critical history because they have become fatigued by the war in Iraq and because no major terrorist attack has occurred on American soil since September 11. But Cocco warns that if the United States does not finish the job in Afghanistan, terrorists will once again take root there—and the United States will experience another colossal terrorist attack. For these reasons, she says, the United States should not abandon the war effort in Afghanistan.

Cocco is a reporter for the *Washington Post*.

W e will never forget, say the bumper stickers, which often bear the image of the smoking Twin Towers superimposed across the red and white stripes of the flag.

But we have forgotten. Or at least we have forgotten that the terrorist attacks of Sept. 11, 2001, demanded that we go to war in Afghanistan.

We Have Forgotten 9/11

This war flares anew, and every day seems to reach some new marker—the most deaths in any year for American and international forces, a tally of U.S. casualties for August [2009] that makes it the deadliest month. Public weariness deepens. CNN [Cable News Network] recently found a precipitous drop in support for the war effort. *The Washington Post* uncovered a more troubling sentiment: A slim majority now says the Afghanistan War wasn't worth fighting.

This is alarming, and inexplicable.

In less than two weeks, the dusty pit in Lower Manhattan that is now a construction site will again serve as hallowed ground, as families of the dead gather at what is, for most of them, their loved ones' grave. New York will hear the doleful sound of bagpipes, and the city will fall silent as the names of the dead are called one by one. The Pentagon ceremony will be less publicized, but no less poignant.

I have often been repulsed by the politicization of 9/11, and by any effort by either political party to gain advantage from its commemoration. Maybe now, though, we need this reminder because too many forget.

Do Not Make a Bad Thing Worse

They forget why we are in Afghanistan—because it was there in a faraway land of poverty, tribal animosities and historic hostility toward outsiders that a sophisticated terrorist network was allowed to take root, to flourish and plot the spectacular attack. Afghanistan today is once again such a cauldron.

That George W. Bush botched the effort there is tragic. The former president duped the nation into believing that an invasion of Iraq was necessary to the fight against terrorism, and devoted far more resources to war there than we expended in the crucial war in Afghanistan—a historic blunder.

But it is no excuse for making another calamitous mistake now.

Americans See the War in Afghanistan as Key to Their Security

Although support for the war in Afghanistan has dropped since 2001, as of September 2009 the majority of Americans still believed that fighting in Afghanistan was helping keep Americans safe.

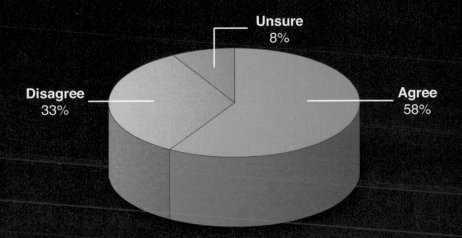

"Do you agree or disagree that the war in Afghanistan is necessary to protect Americans from having to fight terrorists on U.S. soil?"

Unsure
8%

Disagree
33%

Agree
58%

Do Not Abandon Afghanistan Yet

The flagging public support for the Afghanistan effort, Georgetown University terrorism expert Bruce Hoffman says, is a consequence of the Iraq distraction and public fatigue with that war. "Combine that with the economic downturn, the fact that there hasn't been a serious attack since 9/11, and a sense of complacency sets in—which to me vitiates the lessons of 9/11," he said in an interview.

President Barack Obama pledged during his campaign to redirect American resources from Iraq to the effort to wrest Afghanistan from the Taliban's tightening hold and from the grip of the poverty, corruption and regional lawlessness that enabled al-Qaeda to make the country a haven. To abandon Obama's nascent strategy there before seeing if it can work is folly.

And it would be a betrayal.

The activist, liberal Democrats who powered Obama to the Democratic presidential nomination [in 2008] based on his opposition to the Iraq War are the ones who are souring most quickly on Afghanistan, polls show. In May, an early indicator of liberal discontent emerged when the House voted on a war spending measure that 60 members—most of them liberal Democrats—opposed. "I don't think the president can assume that he is going to have the support of the American people in Afghanistan," says Lee Hamilton, president of the Woodrow Wilson International Center for Scholars and a former member of Congress from Indiana. The dissent in the House, Hamilton says, is a "clear danger signal."

> **FAST FACT**
>
> According to the United Nations, from January to June 2009, 1,013 Afghan civilians were killed by Taliban insurgents or other types of fighting. That is 24 percent more than during the same period the previous year.

Obama has been hearing much grousing—some of it from me—from core supporters who are upset at the course of health care legislation, his detainee policy and other issues. These troubles fade when seen in the context of a failure in Afghanistan and a more problematic Pakistan that could emerge from a precipitous American withdrawal.

The author believes that the situation in Afghanistan was made worse by President George W. Bush's decision to invade Iraq before the war in Afghanistan was won.

Failure Means Another 9/11

"You can make the argument that we're in way over our heads, that we're in a quixotic quest—except that there is still al-Qaeda," Hoffman says. "If we don't succeed—and success for me is stabilizing Afghanistan and fixing Pakistan—we're looking at another 9/11."

Obama needs to jolt us out of our complacency, and soon. The Bush administration's fear-mongering was distastefully political. But sometimes we really do have something to be scared about. If we've learned anything from 9/11, we should understand that time is now.

EVALUATING THE AUTHOR'S ARGUMENTS:

Cocco's argument hinges on her belief that if the United States loses in Afghanistan, terrorists will regroup there and use the country as a base to plot attacks against the United States. In your opinion, is this a valid argument? Would a lawless Afghanistan be an asset to terrorists? Or can terrorists plot attacks from anywhere in the world? Explain your reasoning.

The United States Should Send More Troops to Afghanistan

John Nagl

"Building Afghan security forces will be a long-term effort that will require American assistance and advisers for many years, but there is no viable alternative."

In the following viewpoint John Nagl argues that sending more troops to Afghanistan can help win the war there. More American troops can help train more Afghan troops, which are vital to the security of that country. He explains that sending more troops is just one piece of a larger strategy that must have military, diplomatic, and economic aspects. But as in the war in Iraq, sending a surge of troops is the first step to accomplishing these other pieces. Nagl says that Afghanistan can never again be permitted to play host to terrorists—but in order for the country to be stabilized, more American troops will need to be sent and more Afghan troops will need to be trained.

Nagl is president of the Center for a New American Security and author of *Learning to Eat Soup with a Knife: Counterinsurgency Lessons from Malaya and Vietnam.*

AS YOU READ, CONSIDER THE FOLLOWING QUESTIONS:
  1. What has been the effect of thirty years of war in Afghanistan, according to the author?
  2. According to Nagl, how many soldiers—or counterinsurgents—are needed per thousand people to bring peace to a country?
  3. By how many troops does Nagl say the Afghan army must be expanded?

There is an increasingly intense desire to transfer lessons learned from what appears to be a successful counterinsurgency effort in Iraq to America's long-neglected war in Afghanistan. The shift in attention is both laudable and overdue. While Iraq is increasingly secure and stable, Afghanistan is more dangerous than ever. We can certainly do better in Afghanistan than we have over the past seven years of war—but it will require a careful appraisal of what we're trying to accomplish and an appreciation for the resources required to get there.

A strategic review must reflect an understanding of how to apply all the components of American power—not just the military—to achieve our ends. We need an Afghan surge—an increase of troops (including Afghan forces) to enable the application of a population- and oil-spot-security strategy. While additional U.S. troops are necessary, they are not sufficient to achieve success in Afghanistan.

The ends we seek are no sanctuary for terrorists and no regional meltdown.

American goals in Afghanistan have suffered from the most fundamental of all strategic errors: insufficient resources to accomplish maximalist goals. Building a liberal democracy in Afghanistan may be possible, but after 30 years of war, the country simply does not have the human capital and institutions that democracy requires. Creating that human infrastructure is a noble long-term enterprise for the international community, but in the meantime, the United States should focus on more achievable goals: ensuring that terrorists never again have a sanctuary on Afghan territory from which to launch attacks on the United States and our allies, and preventing

Afghanistan from further destabilizing its neighbors, especially the fragile, nuclear-armed state of Pakistan.

While an expanded international commitment of security and development forces can assist in the achievement of these goals in the short term, ultimately Afghans must ensure stability and security in their own country. Building a state, even if it is a flawed one, that is able to provide a modicum of security and governance to its people is the American exit strategy from Afghanistan. Achieving these minimal goals will be hard enough.

In terms of means, we can use U.S. soldiers now, but we must transition to advisers for the long haul. More troops are desperately needed in Afghanistan, but troops alone are insufficient to achieve even limited goals for American policy in Afghanistan over the next five years. Success in counterinsurgency requires the integration of military, diplomatic, and economic assistance to a country afflicted by insurgents; Gen. David McKiernan, the American commander responsible for the International Security Assistance Forces, briefed just such a strategy to a group of scholars visiting Afghanistan in November. Unfortunately, he has not been given the resources required to accomplish his mission.

> **FAST FACT**
>
> A February 2009 *Washington Post* poll found that two-thirds of Americans supported President Barack Obama's decision to send more troops to Afghanistan.

The first requirement for success in any counterinsurgency campaign is population security. This requires boots on the ground and plenty of them—20 to 25 counterinsurgents for every 1,000 people is the historically derived approximate ratio required for success, according to the U.S. Army/ Marine Corps Counterinsurgency Field Manual. That force ratio prescribes some 600,000 counterinsurgents to protect Afghanistan, a country larger and more populous than Iraq—some three times as large as the current international and Afghan force. The planned surge of 30,000 additional American forces to Afghanistan over the next year is merely a down payment on the vastly expanded force needed to protect all 30 million Afghan people.

A U.S. Marine conducts a training session for Afghan soldiers. Expanding and training up to 250,000 soldiers for the Afghan army is key for the U.S. effort in Afghanistan.

The long-term answer is an expanded Afghan National Army. Currently at 70,000 and projected to grow to 135,000, the Afghan Army is the most respected institution in the country. It must be expanded to 250,000, and mirrored by sizable local police forces, to provide the security that will prevent Taliban insurgent infiltration of the population. Building Afghan security forces will be a long-term effort that will require American assistance and advisers for many years, but there is no viable alternative.

How to accomplish these goals? Clear, hold, and build.

Additional troops will be successful only if they are employed correctly. Relearning the classic "clear, hold, and build" counterinsurgency model took several years in Iraq, but to date there are insufficient international or Afghan forces to hold areas that American troops have cleared of insurgents. As a result, the troops have had to clear the same areas repeatedly—paying a price for each operation in both American lives and in Afghan public support, which suffers from Taliban reprisals whenever we "clear and leave."

The alternative requires not just more troops but a different strategy. After an area is cleared of insurgents, it must be held by Afghan troops supported by American advisers and combat multipliers, including artillery and air support. Inside this bubble of security, the Afghan government can re-establish control and build a better and more prosperous community with the help of a surge of American civilian advisers. Since 30,000 more troops won't be enough to secure the whole country, we'll have to select the most important population centers, such as Kabul and Kandahar, to secure first. These "oil spots" of security will then spread over time—a long time. The single most important reason not to think of the new strategy as a surge for Afghanistan is that the term surge is associated with the relatively short-term ramp-up of forces in Iraq. In Afghanistan, the additional forces will be required for the long haul.

Back in September, Adm. Mike Mullen stressed that the need for more security was urgent: "Frankly, we're running out of time," he said. The situation has worsened since then, and the clock is still ticking. While a surge of troops is urgently needed, they must be a component of a new strategy; this ends, ways, and means formulation is one way to think about where we want Afghanistan to go and what it will take to get there.

EVALUATING THE AUTHORS' ARGUMENTS:

Nagl thinks that success can be had in Afghanistan by adopting certain military models that proved useful in Iraq. How do you think the author of the following viewpoint, Eric T. Olson, would respond to this suggestion?

The United States Should Not Send More Troops to Afghanistan

Eric T. Olson

"The first US troops of a 17,000-strong surge are headed to Afghanistan. But to do what?"

Sending more troops to Afghanistan will not improve the situation there, argues Eric T. Olson in the following viewpoint. Although a surge of more troops helped stabilize the nation of Iraq, Olson says factors are at work in Afghanistan that make such an approach unrealistic. An influx of soldiers helped pacify Iraq's cities, which got the rest of the country in line—but very few Afghans live in that nation's cities, so Olson says that approach will not work there. Second, sending more troops will not change the fact that Afghanistan is much bigger and less developed than Iraq, two things that also pose a problem. For all of these reasons, Olson warns against sending more troops to Afghanistan and instead recommends using troops in a way they never have been used before.

Eric T. Olson, "Rethink the Afghanistan Surge," *Christian Science Monitor,* March 17, 2009. Reproduced by permission of the author.

Olson was the operational commander of all coalition forces in Afghanistan in 2004–2005.

AS YOU READ, CONSIDER THE FOLLOWING QUESTIONS:
1. What American state does Olson say Iraq is like? What American state does he say Afghanistan is like?
2. What percent of Afghanistan's population lives in the nation's five largest cities, according to Olson?
3. What makes Olson doubt U.S. soldiers will be able to effectively patrol the Afghanistan-Pakistan border?

With great expectations on their shoulders, the first US troops of a 17,000-strong surge are headed to Afghanistan. But to do what?

Even Secretary of Defense Robert Gates has admitted that these soldiers are being sent without a clear strategy. Several missions have been proposed to turn back a Taliban resurgence. How will 17,000 more troops accomplish any one of them—let alone all?

The beefed-up effort has been fueled by the belief that the successful surge in Iraq can be replicated in Afghanistan.

It can't.

Afghanistan Is Not Like Iraq

I speak from experience: For a year, I was the operational commander for all coalition forces in Afghanistan. Later, I was the deputy director of the Iraq Reconstruction Management Office. The conditions that favored success in Iraq are conspicuously lacking in Afghanistan.

That doesn't mean success there will be impossible—just very difficult. It will require a custom strategy that takes account of hard, local realities.

Some US military officials have warned that what worked in Iraq probably won't work in Afghanistan. Yet Washington's strategy still seems based more on hope than judgment. A closer look at the Iraq surge may provide some needed perspective.

The surge involved 30,000 more troops but its main ingredient was a new operational approach. Instead of "commuting to the war"

In order to counter the Taliban, U.S. strategy must include "living with the people" in the remote regions of Afghanistan.

from bases, soldiers were asked to "live with the people." Their job? Protect Baghdadis from raging violence. Smaller security stations helped soldiers be both more responsive and effective in urban operations and instill confidence in locals. Barriers and checkpoints limited the movement of militants and terrorists. And some nonviolent "soft cleansing" was permitted, transforming some of Baghdad's mixed neighborhoods into single-sect ones, further reducing violence.

But securing the Afghan population is a much more daunting challenge.

Iraq is like New York State: both feature mostly urban populations with dominant capitals. Pacify the Big Apple and you pacify the whole state; pacify Baghdad and you pacify Iraq. But Afghanistan is more like Alaska: both have rural populations with capital cities far removed from large, mountainous regions. Baghdad alone accounts for 7 million Iraqis—about one-quarter of the population. In Afghanistan, barely one-tenth of the population lives in the five largest cities. Because Baghdad is the political and socioeconomic center of the nation, the calming effect of the surge there reverberated across the country. But there is no such city in Afghanistan.

The Wrong Approach

"Living with the people" in Afghanistan will require a completely different configuration. It would require small numbers of US soldiers living in countless small villages, where they'd be unable to support each other in emergencies. And since only about 20 percent of Afghanistan's roads are paved, quick-reaction forces would slow to a crawl, especially in the mountains and in bad weather.

If protecting the population is what's needed to reverse recent Taliban successes, then the best way to do so is through local, small-scale policing where the Taliban has been most successful: in small towns and villages. But the brigades at the heart of the coming surge are insufficient in number and they're not organized, trained, or equipped to do this kind of policing. The mission of the surge force needs to be rethought, with a primary focus on achieving the ability to build effective local security forces.

> ## FAST FACT
>
> A 2009 ABC News/BBC/ARD poll found that just 47 percent of Afghans have a positive opinion of the United States. That is a sharp drop from 2005, when 83 percent of Afghans said they had a positive opinion of the United States.

Cannot Have Military Progress Without Political and Social Progress

As difficult as the security surge will be, the key test in Afghanistan—as it was in Iraq—will be whether political, social, and economic progress is made.

In Iraq, the military surge was accompanied by a political surge, with two key objectives: (1) governmental reform at the national level, and (2) increased capacity in provincial and local governments.

To reach the first objective, US commitments to Iraq were tied to measurable progress. Thus were born the so-called benchmarks,

Americans Oppose a Surge

Because most Americans think the United States is losing in Afghanistan, the majority oppose sending additional combat troops there.

"Do you think we are winning, or not winning, the war in Afghanistan"

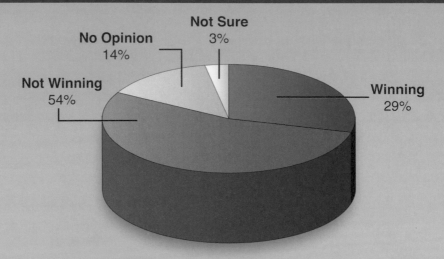

Not Sure
3%

No Opinion
14%

Not Winning
54%

Winning
29%

"Do you favor, or oppose, sending additional combat troops to Afghanistan?"

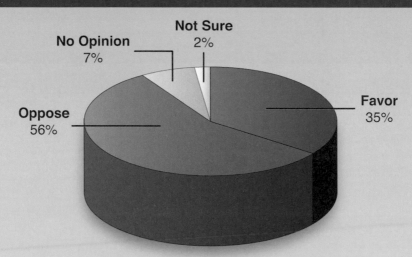

Not Sure
2%

No Opinion
7%

Oppose
56%

Favor
35%

Taken from: Ipsos/McClatchy poll conducted by Ipsos Public Affairs, August 27–31, 2009.

which helped prod Iraq's government to achieve important milestones in political, economic, and social conditions. To date, no similar set of benchmarks has been set for the Afghan government, led by President Hamid Karzai. By handing Mr. Karzai a blank check so far, Washington has undermined the incentives for the central government to make badly needed reforms and win the support of Afghans.

To reach the second objective, the US ramped up the work of provincial reconstruction teams (PRTs). These small, interagency units strengthened local governments while nurturing political and economic institutions at the grass roots. PRT experts proved quite effective at their work, spurring national reform along the way. So far, the plan for Afghanistan does not include a similar PRT surge. To make matters worse, PRTs there are thinly staffed and resourced. Vital expertise is lacking.

It is doubtful that a military surge, even if accompanied by a strong political surge, can be successful without dealing directly with the growing unrest in the Pashtun territories that straddle the border with Pakistan. US authorities have trouble policing the border with Mexico—how can they expect to keep tabs on the Afghan-Pakistani border, which is roughly as long? The challenges in this region are vexing to both nations. Current proposals include sweeping military campaigns, broad international compacts, programs of economic development and aid granted to the governments of both nations, and grand bargains of all types struck between various parties. All these have been tried before. None have worked.

A New Approach Is Needed

What has not been tried (because it has been judged too painstaking) is a systematic effort to address problems in the Pashtun areas on a village-by-village, tribe-by-tribe basis. The tools of such an approach are readily available. They include precisely planned and executed military operations to attack extremist networks without killing innocent civilians, microloans, and microgrants that go directly to meet the needs of local markets and small enterprises (which could avoid the corruption that besets the national government), and reconciliation agreements that target the interests of small groups and recognize the pitfalls associated with applying broad labels ("Taliban," "militant," "drug cartel," and the like). President [Barack] Obama took a step in the right direction this month [March 2009] when he suggested that he would support dialogue with Taliban moderates.

Critical to the success of such an approach will be careful and meaningful cooperation between the Afghan and Pakistani governments and the leadership of the US and NATO [North Atlantic Treaty Organization] headquarters. Washington should also court greater international support from stakeholders who have yet to contribute.

For the secretary of defense to publicly acknowledge that forces are deploying without a clear plan should indicate the difficulties ahead. But the words of another key military leader are worth recalling. At the time of the surge in Iraq, Gen. David Petraeus observed that "hard is not hopeless." "Hard" can become more "hopeful" with a greater—and smarter—effort in Afghanistan, too.

EVALUATING THE AUTHOR'S ARGUMENTS:

Eric T. Olson says that more troops are not the way to go about winning in Afghanistan. If more troops are not the answer, what is? Given what you know on this topic, write two or three paragraphs on what you would recommend the United States do to win in Afghanistan. Or, if you think the situation is unwinnable, explain why.

Forces Should Focus on Helping Afghan Women

Bronwen Maddox

"It's worth making the case for why we should spend money and effort and yes, sometimes, military lives, in defence of women's rights."

In the following viewpoint Bronwen Maddox explains why coalition forces should make helping Afghan women and girls a higher priority. Maddox says that females are treated terribly in that country—they are beaten, murdered, and denied the right to an education simply because of their sex. Maddox reminds readers that one of the reasons America went to war in Afghanistan was to liberate its people from the oppressive Taliban leadership, the same leadership that hosted al Qaeda terrorist Osama bin Laden. Maddox says that wars should not be fought only to help a nation's people, but as long as troops are already there, they should make it a priority to improve people's lives. She concludes that women have an important role to play in Afghanistan, and therefore championing their rights should be viewed as a key part of the war effort.

Maddox is a columnist for the *Times*, a London-based newspaper in which this viewpoint originally appeared.

AS YOU READ, CONSIDER THE FOLLOWING QUESTIONS:
1. Who is Thomas Friedman, and what does he contribute to the author's argument?
2. According to Maddox, what accounted for a large part of the public support for the 2001 invasion of Afghanistan?
3. How many Afghan schools does the author say the Taliban have attacked or closed since 2007? What percentage of these were girls schools?

The trial of Lubna Hussein, the Sudanese journalist sentenced to 40 lashes for wearing trousers in public, was postponed yesterday, a tribute to her gamble in choosing worldwide publicity rather than accepting the sentence, as most do. The Khartoum police promptly found others to beat—the women who had come to protest.

This story resonates all the more in the month of the Afghan presidential elections [August 2009]. It's worth making the case for why we should spend money and effort and yes, sometimes, military lives, in defence of women's rights, in places that barely recognise the concept.

Improving the Lives of Girls and Women

At a tense time in the Afghan mission, it's an unfashionable point to make. On Monday [August 3, 2009], Bill Rammell, the Armed Forces Minister, defined the purpose of the British deployment more tightly than ever. "Our troops are in Afghanistan to keep our country safe from the threat of terrorism," he said. "To prevent al-Qaeda having a secure base from which to threaten us directly."

It's understandable, as stretchers are lifted out of the dust of Helmand [the British-held province of Afghanistan], that ministers should try to retrieve an achievable goal from eight years of tangled ambitions that have ranged from catching Osama bin Laden to setting up democracy and curbing drugs. It makes sense to scale down savagely the aims. After all, in this election, the most pertinent question is how much fraud other countries can countenance and still pronounce the polls "free and fair".

But in all the fervent new realism, I must say, I find it hard to give up the belief that one valuable aim is to improve women's lives in a country where to be born female is to be dealt a horrendously difficult card. Thomas Friedman, the *New York Times* columnist, said two weeks ago: "I find it hard to come to Afghanistan and not ask, 'Why are we here? Who cares about the Taleban? Al-Qaeda is gone . . .'" But after watching a new girls' school opening in the mountains, and "after witnessing the delight in the faces of those little Afghan girls crowded three to a desk waiting to learn, I found it very hard to write, 'Let's just get out of here'."

Afghan women attend a school for young girls in Kabul. Under the Taliban, women were beaten, murdered, and denied the right to an education.

It Is Right to Care About Other People

I'm right with him. Yes, it makes our presence more controversial—not just pursuit of an enemy, not just peacemaking, but nation-building, and in our own image at that. "You don't understand that culture," said one Pakistani Pashtun diplomat. But missions can easily become too leery of saying that, by any standard of humanity, some things are wrong.

A couple of years before the 2001 invasion, I was sitting in Peshawar, Pakistan, with a UN official who dealt with the Taleban across the border in Afghanistan. He had been driven to outright rage by a Taleb that morning who had praised a man for "having done good today" because he had taken his daughters out of school. "These people are evil," he said. Perhaps I should add that he was Dutch; like the Danes, his countrymen are the linchpin of these efforts, refreshingly direct, with their northern European liberalism, in pronouncing on what should be absolutely, globally unacceptable.

> **FAST FACT**
>
> According to UNICEF and the World Health Organization, Afghans face some of the world's worst health conditions. The average life expectancy there is forty-four years. Twenty percent of children die before they turn five. Most people lack access to clean drinking water. Disease, malnutrition, and poverty are widespread, and millions of people depend on food aid to survive.

A good part of public support for the 2001 invasion was horror at the Taleban's cruelty. That wasn't just towards women, of course. But there is no doubt that the stories fired passions, particularly in the US. Khaled Hosseini's novel *A Thousand Splendid Suns*, the tale of an Afghan husband's brutal treatment of his two wives, rocketed into the bestseller lists on that fuel.

Afghanistan's Women Need Our Help

The figures bear out the stories. Afghanistan has the second-highest rate in the world, after Sierra Leone, for women dying in pregnancy or childbirth. Pashtoon Azfar, president of the Afghan

Midwives Association, said last month that women were dying because the culture had not yet decided that their lives were worth saving. US officials say that since 2007 the Taleban and its allies have attacked or closed more than 640 schools in Afghanistan and 350 in Pakistan, and that more than three quarters were girls' schools.

For all the early outrage, women's rights have slid down the agenda as the Taleban have re-emerged and the military task has become bloodier. David Miliband, the Foreign Secretary, argued last week that we should do deals with some Taleban. Very likely he's right to begin to define an exit, but it will demand compromises—such as on women's rights. You can't have it both ways.

Perhaps, something can be salvaged out of this hard new realism. Clare Lockhart, a former UN adviser to the Afghan Government, says that progress is real. The rule that a quarter of parliamentary seats go to women has had a big impact, she says; so have women ministers (at the Treasury and Health). What is needed now, she argues, is a more imaginative focus on jobs for women, say, in the jewellery, fruit and textiles trades. "The real way you get societal shift is when women have economic rights, and assets," she says. At the moment, "while the Taleban feel in the ascendancy" it's better to approach the issue "in a tactical way".

Improving Women's Lives Is a Part of Winning the War

That pragmatism is echoed by David Kilcullen, the senior adviser to General David Petraeus in Iraq and Afghanistan, who suggests that a stronger role for women can counter violence ("The last thing a suicide bomber does is to ring his mother"). He also notes that politicians would provoke outrage at home if they accepted repressive treatment of women without trying to impose conditions for aid.

That may be the best to hope for—that this realism rescues women's rights from the soup of development targets and moves it up the list of priorities. Don't get me wrong: this isn't a pitch for sending forces into Sudan so women can wear trousers. Afghanistan and Sudan are hardly alone in repression of women, or in appropriating Islam to that end, and that is not a case for invasion. Nor am I casually suggesting that we add to casualties by staying until Afghan society is redrawn. But while we are there, it would be a horror of its own if we set aside the goal of improving women's lives or failed to tell Afghan leaders that they should do so.

EVALUATING THE AUTHOR'S ARGUMENTS:

Bronwen Maddox quotes from several sources to support the points she makes in her essay. Make a list of all the people she quotes, including their credentials and the nature of their comments. Then, analyze her sources— are they credible? What qualifies them to speak on this subject? How did she use these quotes to support her main arguments?

The Mission in Afghanistan Must Remain Military

Michael Scheuer

"Economic development, road construction, democracy-building, gender-equality projects, and our other intentions must now be subordinated to three [military] priorities."

The United States must adopt a more military course of action in Afghanistan, argues Michael Scheuer in the following viewpoint. He says in the eight years since the war started, the United States has gotten sidetracked in a massive nation-building project. In addition to defeating the Taliban and destroying the terrorists that hide in Afghanistan, it tried to install a democratic government, help Afghan women, build schools and roads, and undertake other efforts to transform that country into a modern democracy. But Scheuer says Afghanistan is not able to undergo such a transformation—its landscape and culture make such a project utterly impossible. He says the United States lost its focus in Afghanistan: to defeat the terrorists and get out. According to Scheuer, following a military agenda is the only way to avoid getting bogged down in Afghanistan forever.

Michael Scheuer, "Exiting Afghanistan: What Should Have Been a Punitive Expedition Degenerated into Nation-Building. We Must Kill al-Qaeda and Get Out," *American Conservative*, July 1, 2009. Copyright © 2009 The American Conservative. Reproduced by permission.

Scheuer was the chief of the CIA's Osama bin Laden unit from 1996 to 1999. He is also the author of *Marching Toward Hell: America and Islam After Iraq*.

AS YOU READ, CONSIDER THE FOLLOWING QUESTIONS:
1. What problems does Scheuer say America's "light and fast forces" encountered in Afghanistan?
2. Who, according to the author, is the "mayor of Kabul," and what does that term mean?
3. What three priorities does Scheuer say must be the crux of the U.S. mission in Afghanistan?

As America emerges from the eighth winter of the Afghan War, it is appropriate to ask how we got to this point—that is, how we moved from a mandatory punitive expedition to an unnecessary and already lost war—and then ask how we can craft a strategy that will protect U.S. interests.

We Foolishly Ignored History

There is no point in blaming any particular individual or group for the difficult situation we face in Afghanistan. We are all to blame—politicians, military leaders, the media, the citizenry, and perhaps most of all the academy—because we have little knowledge of and less respect for history. It seldom tells you what to do, but history does offer a world-class education in what actions have failed in the past.

After the 9/11 attacks, our perpetually adolescent governing elite crafted a military response in a self-imposed ahistorical vacuum. The plan that emerged played to our military strengths, confronted the enemy as we defined him, and sought a postwar Afghan environment that meshed with our own political values and mechanisms.

We sought to prove the viability of "light and fast forces," few in number and armed with the most modern weaponry, and we sought to prove war could be fought with few casualties on either side and almost none among civilians. We defined the enemy as finite in number, fanatic in temperament, amateurish in military capabilities, and utterly unrelated to any genuine religious faith. Finally, we sought to install a secular democratic political system on a deeply insular, conservative, and tribal Muslim society, and we neglected to establish a nationwide security regime in place of the Taliban law-and-order system we destroyed, apparently thinking the Afghans yearned more for voting than security.

The events of the past 92 months have proven that we should have taken the counsel of history—both ours and the enemy's.

We Underestimated the Enemy

Our light and fast forces were far too small to occupy and administer Afghanistan, a country as large as Texas and home to some of Earth's tallest mountains. History could have told us that the British and Soviet empires failed in prolonged occupations with forces far larger and much more ruthless than ours. Our precision weapons performed well but only when we had enough Marines and soldiers to crawl through the mud and snow to locate targets. In the 1980s, the Soviets found that their most modern weapons systems were no substitute for substantial ground forces. Moscow had up to 120,000 men on the ground, and that force could not even keep open the key Kabul-to-Qandahar highway, let alone achieve anything that could be remotely called victory.

Afghan Mission, cartoon by Keefe, *The Denver Post*, and PoliticalCartoons.com. Copyright © 2009 Keefe, *The Denver Post*, and PoliticalCartoons.com. All rights reserved.

The enemy in Afghanistan turned out to be drawn from an unlimited personnel pool; to be blessed with patience, fortitude, and a strategic sense; to be competent insurgent fighters who learned from their mistakes and adapted to their enemy's method of operation; and to be inspired by a profound religious faith. History could have told us that Alexander the Great, the Queen Empress of India, and several Bolshevik dictators encountered the same formidable enemy and ultimately lost.

Our Attempt to Install Democracy Failed

As for our secular democracy, the Afghan people utterly rejected it because they identified it as a threat to Islam—man's law would replace God's—and as a method for destroying their two-millennia-old tribal society. They wanted nothing from the invading forces except a security regime as effective as the destroyed Taliban system.

FAST FACT

Afghanistan is one of the ten poorest countries in the world and is classified by some organizations as a "failed state." Experts say it will be too much work for the United States to turn it into a functioning nation and so recommend the U.S. mission should be limited to catching and killing terrorists rather than nation building.

So where do things now stand? The position of the U.S.-led coalition is eroding, and the Taliban, al-Qaeda, and their allies have taken the military initiative. Why?

First, we simply do not have enough troops to control the country, let alone defeat the enemy. The situation around Kabul is worrying, and NATO [North Atlantic Treaty Organization] commanders are moving additional troops into the capital region. In eastern Afghanistan, mujahedin [Muslim guerrillas] activities are increasing and new insurgent fighters are regularly entering the country from training camps and safe havens in Pakistan. In the southern Afghan provinces—Qandahar, Nimruz, and Helmand—the situation is particularly poor. The Taliban is on the offensive and is pressing hard on our most important military allies, Canada and Britain. Both are facing declining domestic support and

An Afghan soldier argues with village residents in the remote village of Dahaneh. The villagers do not want government control but prefer to live by the rule of Islam, as they have for generations.

are seeking reinforcements from the NATO countries who have so far contributed little to the Alliance's Afghan operation. Our enemies are well aware of this ebbing public support and, according to al-Qaeda's commander in Afghanistan, Mustafa Abu al-Yazid, the mujahedin intend to "bleed" coalition forces to cause additional dissent. Second, the government of President [Hamid] Karzai is incompetent, corrupt, and shows little or no growth potential. Karzai's opponents' description of him as "the mayor of Kabul" is not far from the mark; he cannot travel in his own country without foreign guards, and his regime could not survive without U.S. and NATO forces. Indeed, it may not be able to survive with them. . . .

We Must Refocus on Military Goals

So how should we move ahead? We must proceed with a sense of urgency and with a set of clear and obtainable goals, neither of which we had at any time since October 2001.

We must accept that time is not on our side. Insurgent forces are growing and being supplemented by Muslim fighters coming from across the Islamic world. Karzai's regime appears to be dealing clandestinely with parts of the Taliban. Heroin production and trafficking are accelerating governmental corruption and funding the insurgents. Traditional Afghan resentment toward foreign occupiers is rising and will increase further as our forces become more engaged in combat in more areas of the country. Moreover, NATO support for the Afghan War is collapsing; the governments of our most important allies—Australia, Canada, and Britain—face the expiration of their Afghan mandates in the next few years and may not be able to persuade their parliaments to grant extensions.

Lacking time and popular support, we must adjust and limit our goals. In terms of the original U.S. aims for Afghanistan, we have lost. Nation-building programs can have very little success until the enemy is utterly defeated, in his eyes as well as ours. Economic development, road construction, democracy-building, gender-equality projects, and our other intentions must now be subordinated to three priorities: (1) eliminating the possibility of the military defeat of NATO; (2) destroying to the greatest extent possible before NATO withdraws those insurgent entities—especially al-Qaeda—that can attack inside the United States; and (3) leaving Afghanistan immediately and entirely once the enemy is severely damaged. . . .

Forget About Nation Building

Today, there is no substitute for the most comprehensive military victory possible over the Islamists in Afghanistan. But such a victory will only be sufficient if we match it with the thorough dismantling of U.S. interventionist policies in the Muslim world, especially Washington's support for multiple Arab tyrannies; and its sovereignty-sapping dependence on Arab oil. The terrorists cannot be dissuaded from their goals by a limited application of U.S. military force; they will not accept a return to a pre-9/11 status quo ante [the way things were before].

Sadly for America, our leaders are still strategizing their hearts out, trying to devise a viable U.S. order of battle for Afghanistan. There is nowhere in sight a Grant, Sheridan, or Thomas[1] to give a telling military victory, and neither is there a political leader in either party with the moral courage to challenge and change the foreign interventionism that ultimately will destroy our Republic.

EVALUATING THE AUTHORS' ARGUMENTS:

Michael Scheuer and Bronwen Maddox (author of the previous viewpoint) disagree on whether helping the people of Afghanistan is a worthy mission. What do you think? Should the United States make helping the people of Afghanistan a priority? Could such efforts make military efforts easier? Or does the United States need to stay focused on winning militarily and not take on the responsibility of changing the whole country? Cite evidence from the texts you have read in your answer.

1. The author is referring to Ulysses S. Grant, Philip Henry Sheridan, and George Henry Thomas, each of whom played a critical role in winning the American Civil War.

Glossary

Af/Pak: Short for "Afghanistan-Pakistan." Commonly used in the names of policies and strategies that take into account dealing with both nations because their problems are inextricably linked.

al Qaeda: The terrorist group led by Osama bin Laden. Al Qaeda operatives carried out the September 11, 2001, attacks on the United States.

Durand Line: The border between Afghanistan and Pakistan. This land is about 1,600 miles (2,640 km) long. The territory along the border is very harsh, made up of mountainous terrain. It is along this area where U.S. troops are spending much time battling the Taliban. In addition to fighting, large amounts of illegal drugs and weapons are smuggled across the Durand Line.

International Security Assistance Force (ISAF): The ISAF is the NATO-led security and development force active in Afghanistan. As of October 2009, it had 67,700 troops from forty-two different countries, including the United States, Canada, most European countries, Australia, Jordan, and New Zealand. An additional 36,000 U.S. troops who are not part of ISAF are serving on Afghanistan's border with Pakistan under Operation Enduring Freedom (OEF).

Islamabad: The capital of Pakistan and its tenth largest city.

Kabul: The capital of Afghanistan.

North Atlantic Treaty Organization (NATO): NATO is an alliance of twenty-eight countries from North America and Europe. The organization offers a forum for member countries to consult on pressing security issues around the world and take joint action in addressing them. NATO runs the International Security Assistance Force (ISAF), the body of coalition troops in Afghanistan.

Operation Enduring Freedom (OEF): The name of the non-NATO U.S. mission in Afghanistan.

the Taliban: The former leaders of Afghanistan. Though the Taliban did not perpetrate the September 11, 2001, attacks, they allowed al Qaeda terrorists who did to train in Afghanistan. The Taliban continue to mount attacks against U.S. and international forces in Afghanistan. They hope to drive out the coalition forces and regain control of the country.

ulema: The body of Muslim clerics.

Timeline of the War in Afghanistan

Editor's Note: The facts contained in this timeline can be used in reports to back up important points or claims.

September 2001
The United States is attacked by nineteen al Qaeda operatives, fifteen of whom are Saudi Arabian. The operatives are found to have been trained in al Qaeda terrorist camps in Afghanistan. President George W. Bush demands that the Taliban, the rulers of Afghanistan at the time, turn over al Qaeda leader Osama bin Laden or face war with the United States.

October 2001
With help from the British, the United States launches Operation Enduring Freedom, a bombing campaign intended to root out al Qaeda and Taliban leaders.

Polls show 94 percent of Americans support the air strikes; 75 percent favor sending in ground troops if necessary.

November 2001
The Northern Alliance—a group of Afghan fighters who are anti-Taliban—breaks through Taliban positions in the city of Mazar-e Sharif. Together, they and coalition forces take the Afghan capital, Kabul.

On November 25, CIA officer Johnny "Mike" Spann becomes the first American casualty of the war when he is killed during a prison uprising in Mazar-e-Sharif, becoming the first U.S. combat casualty of the campaign. American John Walker Lindh is found fighting with Taliban forces.

December 2001
Approximately two hundred al Qaeda fighters are killed in the caves of Tora Bora.

The Taliban are uprooted from the city of Kandahar, but Taliban leader Mullah Mohammed Omar and al Qaeda leader Osama bin Laden escape.

Hamid Karzai, an ethnic Pashtun who leads one of the largest tribes in southern Afghanistan, is sworn in as head of a new interim government.

By year's end, twelve U.S. soldiers have been killed in the war.

February 2002
U.S. forces begin training a new Afghan national army.

November 2002
$2.3 billion in reconstruction funds and an additional $1 billion are approved by the U.S. Congress for expansion of the NATO-led International Security Assistance Force (ISAF).

December 2002
By year's end, sixty-nine coalition soldiers have been killed in the war, bringing the war's casualty total to eighty-one.

January 2003
The United Nations estimates more than 4 million Afghan refugees have been created by the war.

March 2003
The United States begins combat operations in Iraq, a war that will overshadow Afghanistan until 2009.

A CBS News/*New York Times* poll finds that 76 percent of Americans think the war in Afghanistan is going very well or somewhat well; 14 percent think it is going badly or somewhat badly; 10 percent are unsure.

April 2003
NATO takes over command of security forces in Afghanistan.

December 2003
By year's end, 57 coalition soldiers have been killed in the war, bringing the war's total casualties to 138.

October 2004
Elections are held in Afghanistan. Hamid Karzai becomes the nation's first democratically elected president.

December 2004
By year's end, 59 coalition soldiers have been killed in the war, bringing the war's total casualties to 197.

May 2005
U.S. forces are accused of abusing prisoners at detention centers in Afghanistan.

September 2005
For the first time in thirty years, parliamentary and provincial elections are held around Afghanistan.

December 2005
By year's end, 131 coalition soldiers have been killed in the war, bringing the war's total casualties to 328.

May 2006
Anti-U.S. protests erupt in Kabul after a U.S. military vehicle crashes and kills several people.

July 2006
NATO troops take over military operations in the south, where severe fighting persists because of strong Taliban forces there.

September 2006
A CNN/Opinion Research Corporation poll finds that 50 percent of Americans favor the war while 48 percent oppose it.

December 2006
By year's end, 191 coalition soldiers have been killed in the war, bringing the war's total casualties to 519.

May 2007
The Taliban's most senior military commander, Mullah Dadullah, is killed during fighting with U.S. and Afghan forces.

August 2007
The United Nations says that opium production in Afghanistan is at an all-time high since the war began.

December 2007
By year's end, 232 coalition soldiers have been killed in the war, bringing the war's total casualties to 751. The United Nations reports that 1,523 Afghan civilians were killed in 2007.

June 2008
Taliban fighters free twelve hundred prisoners, including four hundred prisoners of war, in an assault on a Kandahar jail. Taliban attacks on coalition forces and civilians intensify throughout the summer.

August 2008
A CBS News/ *New York Times* poll finds that 28 percent of Americans think the war is going very well or somewhat well; 58 percent think it is going badly or somewhat badly; 14 percent are unsure.

December 2008
By year's end, 294 coalition soldiers have been killed in the war, bringing the war's total casualties to 1,045. The United Nations reports that 2,118 Afghan civilians were killed in 2008.

January 2009
Thousands of U.S. troops move into two key provinces in east Afghanistan as part of the strategy of outgoing U.S. president George W. Bush's administration.

February 2009
President Barack Obama orders seventeen thousand additional U.S. troops to be sent to Afghanistan as part of an effort to refocus attention on the war there.

March 2009
Obama announces plans to send four thousand additional troops to Afghanistan.

May 2009
The United States shifts from a conventional strategy to a counter-insurgency one aimed at reducing civilian deaths.

June 2009
U.S. general Stanley McChrystal is put in charge of international troops in Afghanistan.

August 2009
On the 20th, Afghanistan holds its second presidential election since the start of the war, but they are marred by accusations of corruption and fraud.

September 2009
A CNN/Opinion Research Corporation poll finds that just 39 percent of Americans favor the war while 58 percent oppose it—the most since the start of the war.

October 2009
The Obama administration says it will hold off sending new troops to Afghanistan until a legitimate and credible government can be established there.

As of October 19, 418 coalition soldiers had been killed in the war, bringing the war's total casualties to 1,463.

Fifty-three U.S. troops are killed in Afghanistan—the most in any month since the war began in October 2001.

Organizations to Contact

The editors have compiled the following list of organizations concerned with the issues debated in this book. The descriptions are derived from materials provided by the organizations. All have publications or information available for interested readers. The list was compiled on the date of publication of the present volume; the information provided here may change. Be aware that many organizations take several weeks or longer to respond to inquiries, so allow as much time as possible for the receipt of requested materials.

Afghan Women's Network (AWN)
Main Road, Tahmani Watt (Street 9)
Next to Huma Hospital
Kabul, Afghanistan
Web site: www.afghanwomensnetwork.org

AWN is the only umbrella entity for women/gender-based organizations in Afghanistan. It comprises seventy-two organizations and three thousand members in both Pakistan and Afghanistan. AWN is a nongovernmental organization that works to empower Afghan women and ensure their equal participation in Afghan society.

Afghan Women's Organization
789 Don Mills Rd., Suite #312
Toronto, ON M3C 1T5
Canada
(416) 588-3585
Web site: www.afghanwomen.org

This organization was created to address the unique needs of Afghan women and children in the Greater Toronto Area, and even as far as Afghanistan and Pakistan. It is dedicated to assisting Afghan women in all aspects of integration and adaptation to Canadian life; encouraging and motivating Afghan women to participate in and contribute to life in Canada; encouraging and promoting skill-building and development among Afghan women; developing a community support network for women; promoting English language development; and organizing and implementing programs to educate and empower young Afghans to cope with personal, cultural, and social issues.

American Enterprise Institute
1150 Seventeenth St. NW
Washington, DC 20036
(202) 862-5800
fax: (202) 862-7177
Web site: www.aei.org

The American Enterprise Institute for Public Policy Research is a scholarly research institute that is dedicated to preserving limited government, private enterprise, and a strong foreign policy and national defense. It publishes books, including *Democratic Realism: An American Foreign Policy for a Unipolar World* and *The Islamic Paradox: Shiite Clerics, Sunni Fundamentalists, and the Coming of Arab Democracy;* and a bimonthly magazine, *American Enterprise.*

The Brookings Institution
1775 Massachusetts Ave. NW
Washington, DC 20036
(202) 797-6000
fax: (202) 797-6004
e-mail: brookinfo@brook.edu
Web site: www.brookings.org

The institution, founded in 1927, is a think tank that conducts research and education in foreign policy, economics, government, and the social sciences. In 2001 it began America's Response to Terrorism, a project that provides briefings and analysis to the public and which is featured on the center's Web site. It publishes the quarterly *Brookings Review,* periodic *Policy Briefs,* and books on troubled countries, including Afghanistan.

Center for Strategic and International Studies (CSIS)
1800 K St. NW, Suite 400
Washington, DC 20006

(202) 887-0200
fax: (202) 775-3199
Web site: www.csis.org

The CSIS works to provide world leaders with strategic insights and policy options on current and emerging global issues. Numerous reports related to the war in Afghanistan can be downloaded from its Web site.

Council on Foreign Relations
58 E. Sixty-eighth St.
New York, NY 10021
(212) 434-9400
fax: (212) 434-9800
e-mail: communications@cfr.org
Web site: www.cfr.org

The council researches the international aspects of American economic and political policies. Its journal, *Foreign Affairs,* published five times a year, provides analysis on global conflicts, including the one ongoing in Afghanistan.

Hoover Institution
Stanford University
Stanford, CA 94305-6010
(650) 723-1754
fax: (650) 723-1687
Web site: www.hoover.stanford.edu

The Hoover Institution is a public policy research center devoted to advanced study of politics, economics, and political economy— both domestic and foreign—as well as international affairs. It publishes the quarterly *Hoover Digest,* which often includes articles on Afghanistan and the war on terrorism, as well as a newsletter and special reports.

Human Rights Watch (HRW)
485 Fifth Ave.
New York, NY 10017-6104
(212) 972-8400
fax: (212) 972-0905
e-mail: hrwnyc@hrw.org
Web site: www.hrw.org

Human Rights Watch regularly investigates human rights abuses in over seventy countries around the world. It promotes civil liberties and defends freedom of thought, due process, and equal protection under the law. Its goal is to hold governments accountable for human rights violations they commit against individuals because of the latters' political, ethnic, or religious affiliations. It publishes a wealth of information about Afghanistan, including current information, background information, and regular human rights reports.

The National Endowment for Democracy (NED)
1101 Fifteenth St. NW, Suite 700
Washington, DC 20005
(202) 293-9072
fax: (202) 223-6042
e-mail: info@ned.org
Web site: www.ned.org

The NED is a private, nonprofit organization created in 1983 to strengthen democratic institutions around the world through non-governmental efforts. It publishes the bimonthly periodical *Journal of Democracy.*

North Atlantic Treaty Organization (NATO)/International Security Assistance Force (ISAF)
Blvd. Leopold III
1110 Brussels, Belgium
Web site: www.nato.int/ISAF

NATO is an alliance of twenty-eight countries from North America and Europe committed to fulfilling the goals of the North Atlantic Treaty, which was signed in 1949. NATO offers a forum for member countries to consult on pressing security issues around the world and take joint action in addressing them. NATO runs the International Security Assistance Force (ISAF), the body of coalition troops in Afghanistan.

Revolutionary Association of the Women of Afghanistan (RAWA)
PO Box 374
Quetta, Pakistan

e-mail: rawa@rawa.org
Web site: www.rawa.org

RAWA was established in Kabul, Afghanistan, in 1977 as an independent political/social organization of Afghan women fighting for human rights and for social justice in Afghanistan. RAWA continues to fight for freedom, democracy, and women's rights in Afghanistan. It is the publisher of the bilingual (Persian/Pashtu) magazine *Payam-e-Zan*, which means Woman's Message. Its Web site contains news updates and other information pertaining to women's rights in Afghanistan.

UN Development Programme (UNDP) in Afghanistan
1 United Nations Plaza
New York, NY 10017
(212) 906-5317
Web site: www.undp.org.af

UNDP is the United Nations' global development network, helping countries build solutions to the challenges of democratic governance, poverty reduction, crisis prevention and recovery, energy and environment, information and communications technology, and HIV/AIDS. The United Nations Development Programme has been present in Afghanistan for more than fifty years and works to support the people of Afghanistan as they face new challenges and move their country forward.

For Further Reading

Books

Coll, Steve. *Ghost Wars: The Secret History of the CIA, Afghanistan, and Bin Laden, from the Soviet Invasion to September 10, 2001.* New York: Penguin, 2004. Offers revealing details of the CIA's involvement in the evolution of the Taliban and al Qaeda in the years before the September 11 attacks.

Courter, Jeff. *Afghan Journal: A Soldier's Year in Afghanistan.* Scotts Valley, CA: CreateSpace, 2008. Sergeant First Class Courter tells what it was like to be on the front lines in Afghanistan.

Fitzgerald, Paul, and Elizabeth Gould. *Invisible History: Afghanistan's Untold Story.* San Francisco: City Lights, 2009. The authors argue that U.S. policy has placed both Afghans and Americans in grave danger.

Hafvenstein, Joel. *Opium Season: A Year on the Afghan Frontier.* Guilford, CT: Lyons, 2007. Discusses how years after the overthrow of the Taliban, the opium trade has once again become the most important source of revenue in Afghanistan.

Jones, Seth G. *In the Graveyard of Empires: America's War in Afghanistan.* New York: Norton, 2009. A deeply researched and clearly written account of the failures of American policies in Afghanistan.

Neville, Leigh. *Special Operations Forces in Afghanistan: Afghanistan 2001–2007 (Elite).* Oxford, UK: Osprey, 2008. Describes and illustrates the Special Operations Forces (SOF) of the United States and other Allied (Coalition) forces committed to fighting terrorism in Afghanistan since 2001. Readers will find the firsthand accounts into specific operations fascinating.

Rashid, Ahmed. *Descent into Chaos: The U.S. and the Disaster in Pakistan, Afghanistan, and Central Asia.* New York: Penguin, 2009. The author explains how the United States invaded Afghanistan and subsequently refused to commit the forces and money needed to rebuild it. Instead, the U.S. government made corrupt alliances with warlords to impose a superficial calm, while continuing to ignore the Pakistani government's support of the Taliban and other Islamic extremists.

Stanton, Doug. *Horse Soldiers: The Extraordinary Story of a Band of U.S. Soldiers Who Rode to Victory in Afghanistan.* New York: Charles Scribner's Sons, 2009. A riveting account of specially trained U.S. soldiers who were deployed on horseback in the war-ravaged Afghanistan mountains to fight alongside Afghans.

Tanner, Stephen. *Afghanistan: A Military History from Alexander the Great to the War Against the Taliban.* Cambridge, MA: Da Capo, 2009. Offers a good introduction to the fascinating world of Afghan history.

Periodicals

Applebaum, Anne. "Of Course We Can Win in Afghanistan: *If* We're Willing to Pay the Price of Victory," *Slate*, September 15, 2008. www.slate.com/id/2200157.

Bacevich, Andrew. "Afghanistan Surge Is Not Worth the Cost in Blood and Treasure," *U.S. News & World Report*, February 23, 2009.

Biddle, Stephanie. "Is It Worth It? The Difficult Case for War in Afghanistan," *American Interest*, July/August 2009. www.the-american-interest.com/article.cfm?piece=617.

Boot, Max. "How We Can Win in Afghanistan," *Commentary*, November 2009.

Charen, Mona. "Can We Succeed in Afghanistan? Your Nation Building Is a War Crime. Mine Is a National-Security Necessity," *National Review*, August 21, 2009.

Chellaney, Bramah. "An Afghanistan 'Surge' Is a Losing Battle: So Why Is Mr. Obama Betting on It?" *Wall Street Journal*, January 9, 2009.

Diehl, Jackson. "Critical Mass in Afghanistan," *Washington Post*, March 22, 2009.

Economist. "Losing Afghanistan?" August 20, 2009.

Escobar, Pepe. "Pipeline-Istan: Everything You Need to Know About Oil, Gas, Russia, China, Iran, Afghanistan and Obama," AlterNet, May 13, 2009. www.alternet.org.

Fisk, Robert. "Democracy Will Not Bring Freedom," *Independent* (London), August 21, 2009. www.independent.co.uk/opinion/commentators/fisk/robert-fisk-democracy-will-not-bring-free dom-1775229.html.

Fullilove, Michael, and Anthony Bubalo. "The West Can Win in Afghanistan," Brookings Institution, July 28, 2009. www.brook ings.edu/opinions/2009/0728_afghanistan_fullilove.aspx.

Gelb, Leslie H. "How to Leave Afghanistan," *New York Times*, March 12, 2009.

Human Rights Watch. "Afghanistan: Law Curbing Women's Rights Takes Effect," August 13, 2008. www.hrw.org/en/news/2009/08/13/afghanistan-law-curbing-women-s-rights-takes-effect.

Johnson, Thomas H., and M. Chris Mason. "Democracy in Afghanistan Is Wishful Thinking," *Christian Science Monitor*, August 20, 2009.

Jones, Ann. "Ballots and Bullets," *Nation*, August 18. 2009.

Joya, Malalai. "The Big Lie of Afghanistan," *Guardian* (Manchester, UK), July 25, 2009.

Kagan, Frederick. "Why Afghanistan Won't Be Obama's Vietnam," *Newsweek*, February 11, 2009.

Kagan, Kimberly. "Why the Taliban Are Winning—for Now," *Foreign Policy*, August 10, 2009.

Kaplan, Robert D. "Saving Afghanistan," *Atlantic*, March 24, 2009.

Lopez, Ralph. "We Can Win with Jobs, Not Guns, in Afghanistan," *Baltimore Sun*, August 16, 2009.

MacKenzie, Jean. "Afghanistan's Sham Vote," *New York Times*, August 26, 2009.

Noring, Nicklas. "Don't Put Afghanistan in 'Reset' with Russia," RealClearWorld, June 6, 2009. www.realclearworld.com/articles/2009/06/dont_put_afghanistan_in_reset.html.

Peters, Ralph. "Pakistan's US POWs: What's the Plan in Afghanistan?" *New York Post*, February 17, 2009.

Reeves, Richard. "Why Are We in Afghanistan?" RealClearPolitics, February 7, 2009. www.realclearpolitics.com/articles/2009/02/why_are_we_in_afghanistan.html.

Righter, Rosemary. "Don't Sneer at Afghanistan's Wind of Change," *Times* (London), August 25, 2009.

Rosen, Nir. "How We Lost the War We Won: A Journey into Taliban-Controlled Afghanistan," *Rolling Stone*, October 30, 2008.

Rubin, Trudy. "It's Too Soon to Get Out of Afghanistan," *Philadelphia Inquirer*, August 26, 2009.

Simpson, Dan. "Get Out of Afghanistan: We Can't Win There Without Fixing Pakistan . . . and We Can't Fix Pakistan," *Pittsburgh Post-Gazette*, March 25, 2009.

Stewart, Rory. "The Irresistible Illusion," *London Review of Books*, July 9, 2009.

Will, George F. "Time to Get Out of Afghanistan," *Washington Post*, September 1, 2009.

Web Sites

Afghan News Network (www.afghanistannews.net). A collection of news related to Afghanistan from a wide variety of major news sources that is updated regularly throughout the day.

Afghanistan Online (www.afghan-web.com/woman). This site contains articles, poems, and essays describing the plight of Afghanistan's women.

BBC Country Profile of Afghanistan (http://news.bbc.co.uk/2/hi/south_asia/country-profiles/1162668.stm). This site offers maps, statistics, facts, and other current information on Afghanistan's people, land, government, and more.

CIA World Factbook: Afghanistan Page (www.cia.gov/library/publications/the-world-factbook/geos/af.html). This site, maintained by the CIA, contains up-to-date demographic information on Afghanistan. Students will find its maps and facts useful for getting their bearings when doing reports and papers on this topic.

iCasualties. Afghanistan Page (http://icasualties.org/oef). iCasualties tracks the number of dead in global conflicts. On this page it offers up-to-date information on military fatalities broken down by nationality, date, province, and more.

Rethink Afghanistan (http://rethinkafghanistan.com). This site, maintained by the Brave New Foundation, features video clips that argue point-by-point against the war in Afghanistan.

World Health Organization—Afghanistan Page (www.who.int/countries/afg/en). WHO is the directing and coordinating authority for health within the United Nations system. Its Afghanistan site offers demographic information and statistics on life expectancy, morbidity, disease outbreaks, and other health-related news in the country.

Index

Picture Credits

AP Images, 11, 22, 26, 35, 61, 70, 74, 79, 82, 93, 98, 102, 109, 117

Hossein Fatemi/UPI/Landov, 85

Caren Firouz/Reuters/Landov, 55

Hyungwon Kang/Reuters/Landov, 47

Kevin Lamarque/Reuters/Landov, 14

PA Photos/Landov, 43

Omar Sobhani/Reuters/Landov, 37

Steve Zmina, 16, 20, 28, 32, 49, 50, 56, 63, 64, 75, 87, 91, 104